FOR LOVERS ONLY

STEPHEN & JUDITH SCHWAMBACH

HARVEST HOUSE PUBLISHERS
Eugene, Oregon 97402

FOR LOVERS ONLY

Copyright © 1990 by Harvest House Publishers
Eugene, Oregon 97402

Library of Congress Cataloging-in-Publication Data

Schwambach, Stephen, 1948–
    For lovers only / by Stephen Schwambach, Judith Schwambach.
    ISBN 0-89081-865-7
    1. Marriage—United States.   2. Marriage—Religious aspects—Chris-
tianity.   I. Schwambach, Judith, 1949-   II. Title.
HQ734.S415   1991
646.7'8—dc20   90-24022
                                                CIP

Printed in the United States of America.

*To God, who is teaching
us how to love.*

CONTENTS

Secret Number Two
Make Love in the
Garden of Eden!

Doorways

INTRODUCTION

You hold a most unusual book in your hands. As the title suggests, this book is *For Lovers Only*. If you are uncertain about whether or not this includes you, please turn to "Who Should Not Read This Book"! Once you have determined that you are one of the "lovers" for whom this book has been written, please read "How to Get the Most Out of This Book." Then you will be ready to immerse yourself in the first "Secret."

As a glance at the Contents will show, we have divided our book into two major sections, which we call "Secrets." We call them Secrets because, up to now, a comparatively small group of people has been exposed to them.

Both of these major Secrets are divided into a number of short chapters, which we call "Doorways." Each Doorway is so named because as you enter each one, it will lead you into a progressively deeper understanding of the Secret you have chosen to explore.

The first Secret will profoundly increase your potential for intimacy and joy in your personal relationship with one another. The second Secret will profoundly increase your potential for intimacy and joy in your physical relationship with one another.

Should you decide to simultaneously employ both of them in your marriage, you will discover a synergistic effect. As your personal relationship dramatically improves, you will find that your lovemaking becomes vastly more meaningful. As your physical relationship enters new dimensions of wonder, you will find that your day-to-day personal relationship becomes incredibly close and intimate.

The result? Perhaps you will find new meaning in the words of blessing your minister may have spoken over you on your wedding day: "...so they are no longer two, but one." If our book gives your marriage even the smallest nudge in that direction, it will have been worth our efforts.

Although I did most of the actual writing of this book, make no mistake about it—Judy deserves the title of coauthor. For more than 20 years, she has been my constant companion, as together we have refused to surrender to marital mediocrity. She has been my inspiration, my co-explorer, my number-one adviser, and my best friend. Together, we have sought with our whole hearts to discover the wonder God has secreted within His creation of marriage.

You should know, too, that none of the advice in this book has come cheaply. We have dragged ourselves over a thousand miles of broken glass to arrive at the relationship we enjoy today. We do not consider ourselves to be marriage "experts," nor do we have a perfect marriage. To this very day, we have our ups and downs—our difficult times, as well as our times of wonder and delight.

With the apostle Paul, we say, "Not that I have already obtained all this, or have already been made perfect, but I press on to take hold of that for which Christ Jesus took hold of me."[1]

Indeed, the real "secret" to the success of our marriage has been our rock-solid faith in God, and our continuing love affair with His Word. Though we have disappointed Him times beyond counting, He has remained faithful.

The cry of our hearts is for other couples to experience that same faithfulness in their own marriages. It devastates us to see husbands and wives who are bored with each other. It deeply disturbs us to see men and women whose lives together can best be described as "a yawn." There is more—so very, very much more. And we feel compelled to share a portion of it with you, in this book.

Of this we are confident: What you are about to read is solidly based upon the principles of marriage ordained by God Himself. If you put Him first, and then allow Him to lead you as you join us in this adventure, you won't be disappointed.

WHO SHOULD NOT READ THIS BOOK?

Like most authors, we wish everyone could read our book and be helped by the principles within its pages. As our title clearly states, however, this book was written *For Lovers Only*.

And we really mean that. This book is most definitely not for everybody. Who then are the people our book will not help...and may even hurt?

1. Our book is not suitable for children. Approximately half of its content deals specifically with the physical relationship between husband and wife. Although we have gone to great lengths to use language that is in impeccably good taste, our subject matter is nevertheless decidedly adult.

2. Our book has not been written for those men and women who have the gift of remaining single. They have a different set of opportunities for happiness and fulfillment from those we address within these pages.

3. The principles we share in *For Lovers Only* will not work for couples who are only dating each other. The level of total commitment and trust required to take the steps we recommend simply does not exist until a couple is willing to say, "I do."

4. Couples who are living together will likewise find our book unworkable for them, for the reason given in number three. Additionally, however, they have the problem of having entered into a relationship which God cannot bless.

5. People who are uncomfortable with self-examination and correction should not read this book. Our style is directive and requires from the reader a significant desire to grow and, where necessary, to change.

6. This book should not be read by those who may be offended by explicit discussion of sexual matters. At the very least, they must confine their reading to Secret Number One.

7. We urge those who have a critical spirit or an unrealistic negative agenda to refrain from reading any further. It is difficult enough to help a wide variety of couples in areas requiring such delicacy and sensitivity. We freely confess that this work is far short of perfection. Therefore, please do not make the task harder by throwing rocks and shooting deadly arrows.

8. Separated marriages will likely find many of the recommendations in this book simply too dangerous to attempt. They are better advised to first rely on other resources to bring healing to their marriages. Only then will the strategies we share become anything but hopeless fantasies.

9. Married couples who do not wish to "rock the boat" at all should avoid reading this book. It will only upset the equilibrium they have worked so hard to attain.

10. *For Lovers Only* will be most easily implemented by Christian couples. However, its principles will benefit any husband and wife who are strongly committed to each other.

A Word of Clarification

The word, "Christian" is often bandied about rather loosely. We do not use the term in its vernacular sense, however, but in its original biblical meaning.

If you are a Christian, you have confessed to God that you are a sinner and have squarely faced the penalty for your sins, which is eternal separation from God in a literal place called hell. Furthermore, you believe that God loved you so much that He sent to this earth His only Son, Jesus Christ, to die on the cross in your place, paying for your sins with His own life. Because Jesus is God, you believe He then rose from the dead, returned to heaven, and is even now preparing a place for you to live with Him eternally when your life on this earth is through.

Although you strive with all your heart to obey God and please Him in everything you do, you are painfully aware that your good deeds do not have the power to take you to heaven. Instead, you know that you will live with God forever solely because of the sacrifice of Jesus Christ on the cross in your behalf. Nor have you kept your belief to yourself. You have specifically asked Jesus to be your Savior, and you have informed others of your decision to become a disciple of Christ.

If all of this applies to you, then you match the biblical definition of a Christian. As a result, you have God's Holy Spirit living inside you. It is His powerful working within your life that will enable you to implement any or all of the principles in this book, should you elect to do so.

If the above description does not apply to you, you have a choice to make. Certainly, you may choose to return this book to the shelf, since some of its secrets may be outside the reach of your current capacity. Or ... you can increase your capacity.

In other words, you can begin now to investigate the claims of Christ. Believe me, if you search with your whole heart, you are going to love what—and whom—you find.

I encourage you to find a church that is absolutely faithful to the Bible and that is not ashamed to say so. It will be especially helpful if you can find a church in your area that offers a "Seeker's Service," specifically designed to meet the needs of people who want to hear Christianity presented in terms that they can identify with and can easily understand.

An alternate approach is to start calling churches until you find one that will send an evangelism person or team to your home to answer your questions about Christianity. If the first few churches you call don't seem to know what you are talking about, you haven't found the right one yet! Don't become discouraged—keep looking. God will help you to connect with the right church.

Once you have completed your search and have accepted Jesus Christ as your personal Savior, the examples we share in *For Lovers Only* will take on new and exciting dimensions. If we are then able to serve you and your Christian spouse with this book, Judy and I will be deeply gratified.

How to Get the Most Out of This Book

We strongly urge you to explore the two Secrets of this book in the order we have presented them. With some books, you can skip around and read whatever catches your eye. In fact, the last book I wrote, *Tough Talk to a Stubborn Spouse*, was specifically designed to work that way.

But not this one. If you read a little here and a little there, you will become quickly confused, and there is even a good chance that you could end up being offended.

Obviously, you purchased this book, and we recognize your right to read it in any manner you choose. But for your sake, please trust us on this one. Take it Secret by Secret, Doorway by Doorway, in the order we have presented them. You'll be glad you did!

How to Approach the First Secret

The first Secret is entitled, "Do All Your Quarreling in One Hour a Week!" The concept sounds radical and unworkable, but if you'll keep reading with an open mind, you will find that the farther you go, the more sense it will begin to make.

So our advice is to journey all the way to the end of the first Secret before you decide whether or not to adopt this strategy in your marriage. If on completion you are excited about the concept, your next step is to ask your spouse to read the entire Secret as well. As you will be able to see when you get into it, the only way this peace-giving recipe will work is if both of you are totally committed to its implementation.

Having said that, however, let me quickly add that you do not have to adopt the entire system. After you have both read it through, you may elect to use only the parts that fit your personalities or situation.

How to Approach the Second Secret

The second Secret must be approached entirely differently from the first. As you can readily see from its title,

"Make Love in the Garden of Eden!" this Secret is designed to enhance your mutual enjoyment in married lovemaking. The sensitive nature of this topic requires that we take considerably more space than we did for the first Secret to prepare you for our approach.

Because of the private, personal nature of sexuality, some Christians tighten up at any mention of the subject. To them, anything beyond the vaguest reference to the physical side of marriage is in decidedly poor taste. We will call these our "Type X" readers. If you identify a little more closely with this first category than with the next two we mention, you will want to skip the second Secret altogether. It will only upset you, and we do not want to have that effect upon you for anything in the world. You are precious and valuable in the sight of God, and we honor you for the sensitivity of your Christian convictions. There is, after all, plenty of room for enormous variety within the body of Christ.

On the other hand, some Christians are thrilled at the prospect of gaining new perspective and picking up fresh, creative ideas for their physical relationship. "All right!" they respond. "It's about time!" It would be impossible for us to offend this group of people—unless we merely re-hashed material with which they were already familiar, and therefore failed to live up to our promise to expand their sexual horizons. We will call these our "Type Y" readers.

If you are a "Type Y," it is important for you to begin at the beginning, as we have already mentioned. The danger is that you "Y's" will be tempted to get to the "good stuff." Please resist this temptation! Although you will not be offended by the content of any of these Doorways, it is nevertheless vital that you lay a strong, biblical foundation for their implementation. To enter the final Doorways of this Secret outside of their Christian context is to invite danger. Please allow us to set the biblical boundaries for you. Only after you have learned the location of the pitfalls is it safe for you to run freely through the fields!

The rest of you, obviously, will fall somewhere in between these opposite poles: our "Type Z's." You recognize your need for Christian teaching on sexuality, certainly, but you suspect you may have your limitations on what you may want to hear discussed. Yes, you want to be "stretched" sexually... but not too far!

Fair enough. So here is what we recommend for you "Z's." Start with the first Doorway and read through it with this question uppermost in your mind: "Am I comfortable with what I have read so far?" If the answer is "Yes," then you may proceed to the next Doorway. But if at any point, even in the midst of passing through one of these Doorways, your answer is "No," or "I'm not sure," then you have read far enough. It is time to stop. Curiosity may tempt you to read on "just to see what these people have to say," but at that point it would be wrong of you to do so.

Which of these categories has the best marriage: the "X,'s," the "Y's," or the "Z's"? The truth is, all of them can be equally good, both in the eyes of God, and in terms of their mutual happiness with each other. God has created all kinds of people, and all kinds of sexual expressions. As long as we stay within the boundaries of His Word, He pronounces everything He has created "Good!"

Who is the better gourmet: the person who uses no pepper, the person who uses a little pepper, or the person who coats everything he eats with a black blanket of pepper? It's an irrelevant question, isn't it? Nobody is right, and nobody is wrong. A fondness for, or avoidance of pepper has nothing to do with who is the best gourmet. Our God has created a variety of taste buds!

What we are telling you is that Secret Number Two contains plenty of "pepper." With each consecutive Doorway, we sprinkle on a little more. If you don't care for pepper and someone tells you that a particular dish contains a lot of pepper, wisdom dictates that when offered that dish, you respond with, "No, thank you." On the other hand, if you do like pepper, then you can continue to eat until your mouth gets warm. At that point, it is time to lay down your fork, smile, and say, "Thank you very much. Now, I'd like a glass of water." Finally, there will always be some people who will say, "This is all very good, but I'd like more pepper, please. What? You're all out? Awwwww!"

Who's right and who's wrong? Once again, it is an irrelevant question, isn't it? Our God has created an amazing variety of legitimate sexual tastes!

Let's change analogies and talk clothing. Which clothing is better: big clothing, small clothing, or medium-size clothing? Well, that all depends, doesn't it, on which clothing fits! How foolish it would be for you to find a shirt that fit you perfectly, but reject it because it wasn't "big" enough! "Big" isn't necessarily better. It's only better if you are bigger!

Just as God has made people of all sizes, He has made people of all sexual temperaments. Furthermore, He loves us all. The person who wears a sexual size "9" is neither better nor worse than the person who wears a sexual size "13." They are just different, that's all. Suppose you were a perfect size "9," but felt you were missing something, and insisted on wearing a size "13." What a mistake that would be! You would end up looking baggy and disheveled, and feeling quite ridiculous. For you, sexual size "9" is exactly where it's at.

By the same token, it would be horribly unfair of you to insist that size "9" is the only level of sexuality that is acceptable. You would be wrong to point your finger at a size "13" couple and ridicule them for being two sizes away from what is "right." If they attempted to jam their generous bodies into your size "9" outfit, they would feel restricted and highly uncomfortable.

The person who feels best wearing an "XXL" (extra-extra-large) level of sexuality is no better or worse than the person who feels best wearing an "S" (small) or an "M" (medium). Therefore, since God has created people of every description, we have stocked this section of our book accordingly, with all sexual sizes. Once you find the sexual "size" that fits you, stop. You need go no further. Put on the "outfit" that best fits you, and wear it with thanksgiving.

If, however, against our advice, you insist on browsing through the rest of the rack, please do not become offended because we also carry size XXXXXXXL! It would be wrong of you to point a finger at the couple who finds sexuality that "big" perfectly comfortable. Don't mock them, saying,

"Have you seen *this* shirt? Ha! What a tent!" Rather, please have the decency to respect the simple fact that God has made us all different.

Certainly it is important to remember, too, that you and your spouse do not wear the same "size." You have different personalities, different pasts, and different needs which may vary from time to time. Therefore, your "size" as a couple will differ from either of your "sizes" as individuals—with much sensitivity required on both your parts!

Why have we chosen to carry such a wide variety of sizes? Because for too long, many Christians have been unable to find anything in Christian literature that fits them sexually. Or, even when they were able to find a few items, they wished they had more of a selection to choose from. This book is our attempt to begin to meet the needs of a wide variety of couples, but without in any way compromising Christian standards.

We hope you will agree that it is about time.

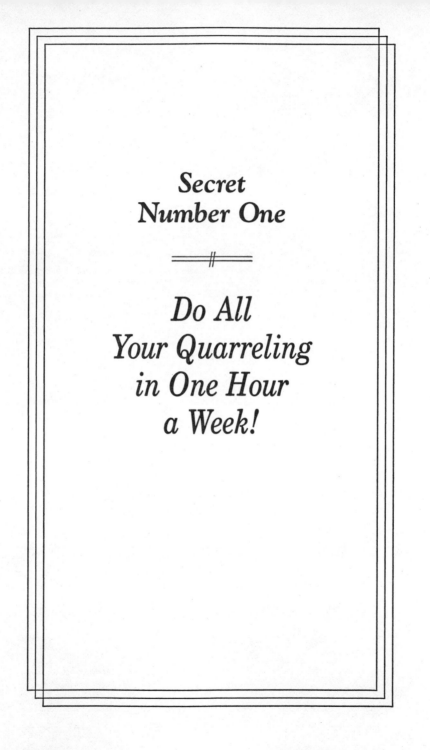

Secret
Number One

Do All
Your Quarreling
in One Hour
a Week!

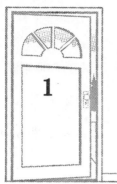

Life's Too Short to Waste!

T he issue is time. How much time can you beg, borrow, or steal each day to devote exclusively to one-on-one time with your mate? Not much. Try though you might to rearrange your priorities, the amount of time you can scrape together for each other is shockingly small.

So here's the sobering question: How many of those precious minutes do you want to squander fighting with each other? Let's face it: When you figure in four or five exchanges of angry words, all those hurt looks, the silent treatment, two or three sob sessions, and the time it takes to go on an effective pout, a serious spat can run on for days. The fallout, when things are somewhat better but still strained, can last for weeks.

Sure. Because you're lovers, you eventually make up, and things are great again . . . until the next time. But you know what? Life's too short for that. It really is.

One of these days, much sooner than you want to face, one of you is going to be sitting beside the deathbed of the other, holding a frail, clammy hand. You'll look into each other's misty eyes during those aching, final hours, and the memories will flood through your grieving minds in a raging torrent.

You will not regret a single dreamy walk you took together in the park. You will not regret the time you stayed up so late talking and holding each other that you were both zombies at work the next day. You will not regret all the times you made love and let the housework go.

But I'll tell you what you will regret. You will regret the thousands of hours that you spent fighting over nothing.

Oh, at the time it seemed like a big deal. At the time, you were both so worked up over those burning issues that you would have thought the fate of the free world hung in the balance. But on the last day you spend with your lover on this earth, you will see all the things you fought over for what they really were: nothing. Absolutely nothing.

On that day you won't care who got in the last word. On that day it won't matter one whit which of you finally got his way. On that day you won't even be able to remember what started 99 percent of the fights. All you'll remember is that it was priceless time irretrievably, foolishly lost.

Wouldn't it be great if you could cut it out right now? Wouldn't it be fantastic if you knew a way to eliminate your lovers' quarrels once and for all? Think of it: no more coming home wondering what's waiting for you on the other side of the front door, no more lovely dinner plans ruined by bickering, no more romantic atmospheres destroyed by an ill-timed complaint.

Sound impossible? It is—for everyone but two absolutely committed lovers. But if that's who you really are, there is a way, and it really works. Let us show you how.

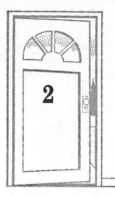

2

Carve Out a Single, Quality Hour

———— # ————

Pick an hour that is good for both of you, when you are at your mutual best. Do you like to get up early in the morning, while your husband prefers to stay up late? Then don't schedule your hour for either of those times. It will be bad for one of you. Schedule it somewhere in between— before you start to wind down, but after your lover has rubbed the sleep out of his bleary eyes.

"But that's not nearly enough time!" you may protest.

Sure it is. Believe me, in one hour's time, you and your spouse can say enough to keep one another busy for the entire week! And that's the real issue. What point is there in loading your husband up with more than he can handle in a reasonable length of time? Other than getting it off your chest, you will have accomplished little or nothing. No one can work on everything at once.

Just be sure that you bring up the problems you want to address in their order of importance. Deal with the most pressing issue first. If there is time, deal with the second most important issue next, and so on.

It is understandable that you would like to solve all your problems immediately, but that is not how life works. Each issue is resolvable, but in its own time. You can work on it in advance all you like, and you can complain until everyone is weary of hearing about it, but nothing will change until the time is right. Recognizing this fact of life will allow you to deal with your problems in their proper priority, with genuine patience.

What do you do with the leftover problems that you couldn't get to within a single hour? Unless one of them is a true emergency, save them for next week's hour appointment! It is far better to give your spouse two or three areas each week that he might actually work on, than to overwhelm him with nine or ten that may cause him to throw up his hands in despair of ever being able to keep up with your demands.

3

Share Your Needs Instead of Your Complaints

━━━━ # ━━━━

*I*f by now you're remembering the last time you went at it toe-to-toe with your mate, you may have a lot of difficulty imagining how you can accomplish very much in a single hour.

You're right, of course. When you confront your spouse with a major problem, you usually open a can of worms that takes from here to doomsday to sort through and clean up.

That is why I am going to recommend that you totally change your method of dealing with marital problems. Almost hidden away within the Book of Ephesians is a single verse of Scripture that can revolutionize your marriage. At first, it seems so unrealistic that most people tend to ignore it, put it on hold for future reference, or attempt to explain it away. But the profound wisdom of these 31 words hold within them the potential for the dawning of a new day in your relationship:

> Do not let any unwholesome talk come out
> of your mouths, but only what is helpful for
> building others up according to their needs,
> that it may benefit those who listen.[1]

23

Several years ago, Judy and I sensed what this single verse of Scripture could do for the joy and harmony of our marriage. So we both committed it to memory. I wish I could tell you that it was as easy to obey this verse as it was to memorize it!

Unfortunately, it was not. We have both struggled as hard as you probably will in our attempt to implement its radical implications in all of our conversations with one another. In our hurt or frustration, we have often cast this precious principle aside and simply let each other have it with both barrels. But in the aftermath of our weakness, we have had to sheepishly admit that God's way is better— much, much better.

Therefore, this vital hour that you spend together once each week is not meant to be a gripe session. It is a *need-sharing* session. And between the two there is all the difference in the world.

Listen to a typical gripe:

> If there's one thing I can't stand about you,
> it's the way you constantly correct me when
> we're with other people. What makes you
> think you're so smart? Don't you think I have
> any feelings? How would you like it if I kept
> putting you down every time you opened your
> mouth?

Now here's the same gripe, but this time presented as a need:

> Darling, your support means so much to
> me—especially when we're with other people.
> I know that sometimes when I'm telling a
> story, you and I remember the facts

differently. But I'm really sensitive to public
correction. It hurts me, embarrasses me. From
now on, if you think I'm making a mistake,
would you please wait to tell me until we're
alone? It would really help me to relax and
enjoy the evening.

Wow! What a difference! The first approach makes your
husband feel as though he is under attack. When a human
being thinks he is being attacked, what is his automatic
response? To defend himself!

"Wait a minute!" your husband is going to protest when
he hears the first approach. "All I'm doing is making sure
people hear facts, not lies! Do you know what your problem
is? You're so insecure that you can't handle correction.
What you need to do is grow up!"

Oh yeah. It's gonna take a whole lot longer than an hour
to extricate yourselves from that one. But consider the
alternative. In the second approach, you change your focus
from his error to your need. Since you never once accuse
him of doing anything wrong, you haven't triggered his
defense mechanism—quite the reverse. By showing him
how vulnerable you are, you have triggered his sense of
protection. Instead of defending *himself*, it makes him
want to defend *you*!

With this approach you may hear something more like
this:

Do I do that? Honey, I'm sorry. I just didn't
realize it affected you that way. I wouldn't
intentionally hurt or embarrass you for
anything in the world! Hey—from now on, you
tell it the way you see it, and I'll keep my big
trap shut!

Isn't that the response you want? Then you're going to have to learn the approach it takes to get it. Sure, it will be difficult at first. But the harder it is for you to change, the more proof you have of just how badly you need to do so!

What we are advising is that the radical advice of Galatians 6:1 actually be obeyed: "Brothers, if someone is caught in a sin, you who are spiritual should restore him *gently.*"

It's easy to be harsh. All you have to do is nail the sin and the sinner with the haughty rush of your righteous indignation. Gentleness is much tougher. It requires calming down, getting hold of your emotions, and actually thinking the situation through from the other person's point of view before you ever speak!

But it is also more godly. That's why Paul pleads with Christians: "Be *completely* humble and gentle; be patient, bearing with one another in love."[2]

Now do you see why you want to wait to confront each other until after you've had a chance to think the problem through? You need the time to get your words right! Almost nobody is able to be this caring and considerate toward the "guilty" party right away—especially when the hurt goes deep.

Let's try another example. Since you were the one who began the hour by sharing one of your concerns, it's your husband's turn. Which approach do you think will work best on you? Suppose he clears his throat and says:

> Do you know what I think? I think you love
> the kids more than you love me. Monday
> night is a prime example. I kept begging you
> to come into the bedroom with me before we
> were both too tired to do anything but sleep.
> Instead, you put me off until 11:30 helping

them with their homework, fixing lunches,
and reading them bedtime stories. I'm left
playing second fiddle around here, that's all.
Either that, or you've gone frigid on me in the
last six months!

So how's your blood pressure? You've been attacked.
Will you get just a tad defensive? You bet you will!
Shaking with righteous indignation, you'll let him have
it right between the eyes:

I can't believe you said that. Of all the self-
centered...Hey, Mister! If you wanted to go to
bed early Monday night, why didn't you help
me with the kids? They're yours, too, you
know! Instead, you sat there watching your
stupid football game while I did everything all
by myself. And as for "frigid!" Are you
forgetting last Saturday afternoon? You call
that "frigid?" Well, you'd better remember it,
Bucko, because it's going to be a long time
before you see anything like *that* again!

Hmmmm. Maybe there's a better way. What if your
husband approached you like this, instead:

Darling, I still can't get last Saturday
afternoon out of my mind. You were fantastic.
You've ruined me! I can't wait for the
weekends to experience you like that. I know
things are hectic on school nights, but I'm
desperate for you, Darling! Do you think we
can come up with a way to get the kids down
and us in bed while we still have enough

energy for each other? I could have died
Monday night when they were still up and it
was nearly 11:30!

A leeedle bit different feel to that one, huh? Do you
think your response might be different as well?

My poor baby. Was Saturday afternoon too
much for you? Maybe I shouldn't have come on
so strong, do you think? Just teasing! Oh,
Honey, I wanted you Monday night, too! I'll
tell you what. If you'll help me with the kids
tonight, we'll try for lights out at 9:30. That
is, if you think your heart can stand it! How
does that sound?

Sounds good to me. And it will sound good to him...
because what he said to begin with sounded good to you!
Are you starting to get the picture? It makes a lot of
sense, doesn't it? Sure, it will take some getting used to—
so does changing from a '79 Volkswagen to a brand-new
Cadillac. But most people find that they are willing to
make such sacrifices.
"What if I can't come up with a way to word my complaint positively?" you might be wondering. Every legitimate complaint can be rephrased as a need. If you cannot
come up with a way to express your complaint as a need,
you had better think twice about saying anything. After
all, if there is no need, why register a complaint?

It's Easier to Share Your Need Than to Prove Your Mate Wrong

4

The great thing about sharing your needs rather than your complaints is you don't have to try to prove that your position is right and your wife's position is wrong.

If you tell her, "It was very inconsiderate of you to give me such a small glass of water at dinner last night," the burden of proof is on you. You've labeled her "inconsiderate," and now you have to back it up. You're going to have your hands full, too, because very few women will admit to being inconsiderate without putting up a ferocious defense.

What you would love for her to say is, "You're right, Sweetheart. The glass of water I gave you last night was too small. I promise to do better in the future."

But that's not what you're gonna hear. Instead, you're going to get an earful of this:

> *Me* inconsiderate! What about you? There
> you sat on your chair like an impatient
> customer at some restaurant, while I had to
> set the table all by myself! Your glass was the
> same size as everybody else's. If you wanted a

bucket to drink out of, why didn't you drive down to the feed store and get one for yourself?

See what I mean? Here's a better way to handle it. When it's your turn to speak, tell her:

Darling, your lasagna was great last night, as always. I love the way you make it with all those extra spices. There's nothing worse than bland lasagna. In fact, your spicy lasagna is so good that I eat twice as much and get twice as thirsty! Do you think you could give me one of those big iced tea tumblers the next time you serve that delectable dish?

Can you tell the difference? Your first approach puts all the pressure on you. You're stuck trying to prove her inconsiderate. Before it's all over, you're going to need a judge, 12 jurors, and a better attorney than you can afford to make your case stick! (You really should have helped her set the table, you know.)

This business of attempting to prove each other wrong is a long, drawn-out, entirely unsatisfactory affair. After all, what do you care who takes the rap? All you want is a tankard of water with your lasagna, right? Then forget the blame. Tell her you're thirsty because her lasagna is so good (if it's the truth!), and she's not going to fight you.

Why? Sure, you complimented her, and that was wise because she deserved it. But that's not what made it work. It worked because you shared your need rather than your complaint. If you doubt that, let's try the old compliment-complaint-compliment approach, otherwise known as the "Sandwich Method."

Suppose you tell her,

> Honey, your lasagna was delicious last
> night! The only problem I had with the meal
> was that you gave me such a small glass. I
> had to keep asking people to pass the water
> pitcher, and twice I had to go into the kitchen
> for more ice. Other than that, the meal was
> delicious. Your spicy lasagna is one of my all-
> time favorite dishes!

Your wife will enjoy your first compliment until she hears your complaint. Then her expression will change. By the time you get to your second and third compliments, you'll be wasting your breath because she won't be listening.

Think about it. If somebody squirted a dropperful of acid in the middle of an otherwise delicious scrambled egg, what would you focus on? Would you eat the whole thing because the edges were good?

A complaint is the acid of lovers' conversation. When you pour one on, it causes your husband or wife to react with pain. It eats away at your spouse for a long time afterward. And it hurts so much that they are likely to throw acid right back on you.

On the other hand, you are—indisputably!—the only one who is qualified to say whether or not you are thirsty. Don't find a fault—share a need! Your spouse will have a much easier time meeting your need than they will accepting your blame.

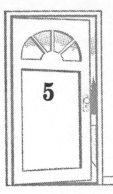

Don't Imply Blame When You Share Your Need

5

This is important: When you share your need, don't imply that you are needy because your spouse was negligent. Don't say, "Tuesday morning I tried to get dressed and couldn't find any clean socks. I need you to stay current with the wash."

You shared a need, all right, but I guarantee that your wife received it as a complaint. Whatever you do, don't share your need as though any wife who was paying attention would have noticed the problem and kept it from happening. When you do that, you demonstrate that you are still harboring some of that anger you were supposed to have eliminated before the sun went down![1]

When you share a need, don't transfer any blame to your spouse. This holds true even though when you and your wife divided up the household duties, she may have assumed responsibility for the laundry. How do you handle your need for clean socks? Like this:

> Honey, I don't know how you keep up with everything—I really don't! You work full-time, then you come home and manage this

household better than most women who don't
have jobs. Do you know what my "need" is?
Clean socks. You're doing such a great job
that I don't even want to bring it up!

So I got to thinking. I go through so many
socks in such a short time, that I should
probably go out and buy another dozen pair.
What do you think? Is that enough? Asking
you to keep up with the few pairs I've got is
just ridiculous.

Do you see what that does? It puts the responsibility all
on you. There isn't a complaint against your wife to be
found, hidden or otherwise, anywhere among those ten
carefully chosen sentences.

How do you achieve that? You put yourself in her place—
and not just a little bit, but all the way. You ask yourself,
"How is it going to feel to her to get a request for clean
socks? With everything she's got going, could this be the
straw that breaks the camel's back? Then how can I lighten
her load, rather than add to it? How can I solve my problem without simultaneously creating one for her?"

The Issue Is Your Relationship—Not Your Socks

6

I f you think things through from your wife's perspective as I've just suggested, it's going to take some time. How much time? That depends on you. It took me 15 minutes to come up with the 105 words in those ten sentences.

"Come on," I can just hear you chuckling right about now. "All of this over a pair of socks? Get real!"

You're right, of course. Clean socks aren't worth this much attention. But I'll tell you what is: the fragile tenderness and intimacy you share as lovers.

So let me turn the tables on you and reword the question this way: "Are you willing to destroy that rare, sweet communion you enjoy with your darling over a pair of socks?"

No—a thousand times no. And until we see it clearly, that's the mistake we keep making again and again in our marriages. Without thinking, we fling out our complaints about running out of clean socks, not carrying in the groceries, drippy faucets that haven't been fixed, and 60-second foreplay that wouldn't be enough time to warm up a leftover bowl of beans in the microwave.

But the issue isn't socks, sacks, sinks, or sex. The issue is your relationship. You are lovers! If you've been married many years, you've had to pay a big price to get where you are. Who in his right mind would not be willing to spend 15 minutes of creative thinking in order to preserve the closeness that you have sacrificed so much to achieve since the day you said "I do"?

7

The Payoff Is Awesome!

When you finally learn to rethink all of your complaints until you can express them as personal needs, a new day will have dawned in your relationship. If you have never experienced it, there is no way for me to describe to you how it feels to go six months without hearing a single criticism from your spouse.

You open up to each other like never before because, for the first time in your marriage, it's safe to drop your guard. No matter what you do or say, you don't have to flinch. Your spouse isn't going to lash out at you for it. The security of that certain knowledge is so rare and so sweet that it can literally make you weep for joy.

Even so, the idea of giving up your right to complain is a frightening thing. Your greatest fear is that your mate will take advantage of you. But once you both make the leap, the opposite takes place. A marriage free of faultfinding is so happy and so liberating that neither of you is willing to do anything that will mess it up!

Of course your marriage will never be perfect, and neither will be your adherence to these principles. But when you become a little lax and suffer the consequences, you will always know the steps to take to get your marital joy back on track.

8

Be Prepared to Explain Your Needs

I f all this so far sounds like pie in the sky, it's time to insert this important qualification: Although you will not have to *defend* the needs you share with your spouse, you most certainly should be prepared to *explain* them.

The very fact that this need of yours is going unmet probably means that your lover just doesn't understand it to begin with. Or maybe he just needs to be reminded of the reason for your need because it is so different from his way of perceiving the world.

Since you have a good, balanced relationship, your husband is probably your opposite in many ways. So when you use one of your turns during the hour to tell him, "I need you to go shopping with me on Saturdays," I promise you he's going to want to know why! And you'd better be ready with a well-thought-out answer!

Before you ever mention it to your spouse, you need to ask yourself, "Is this my need, or someone else's? Do I want my husband to go shopping with me primarily because Carolyn's husband goes shopping with her?"

Also ask yourself, "Is it possible that the request I'm making is actually a substitute for something else I really need?" Perhaps your real desire is to spend more time together on the weekends. In that case, since time is limited, you may want to ask yourself if a shopping mall where you are surrounded by thousands of strangers is really how you want to spend that precious time. If you can carve out only three hours to spend together next Saturday, you may prefer to go for a picnic and a walk in the park with your husband—and do your shopping later with a girlfriend!

On the other hand, you may really need your husband to go shopping with you on Saturdays. If so, you are going to have to help him understand why—especially if your husband detests shopping! Do not expect him to read your mind. Do not expect him to just "intuit" it like another woman may be able to do. And above all, do not fall into the trap of thinking that if he really loved you he would want to go shopping, no questions asked!

Let me show you what I mean: Suppose your husband thinks the greatest gourmet delicacy on earth is a nice, juicy brain sandwich, but your stomach rebels at the idea of chewing and swallowing something that a 400-pound hog has been using to think with. Wouldn't you need a lot of explanation and a heap of ketchup if he suddenly told you he "needed" you to eat a brain sandwich along with him? Don't you think it would be unreasonable of him to insist that if you really loved him you would bite that brain?

So okay, none of this "I don't feel loved!" pity-party stuff. Sure, you're loved. You're lovers, remember? But let's face it. Just like it would be difficult for you to sink your teeth into the mushy mind of a swine, going shopping with you is going to require your husband to make a sacrifice.

So sell him on it! What you've got to do is hook his already strong desire to please you by showing him exactly how much it means to you to have him accompany you to the Galleria this Saturday.

> I can't begin to tell you what it would mean to me if we could go shopping together this Saturday afternoon. Remember last Christmas when you went along to help carry Jerry's bike out to the car? When we walked into that toy store hand-in-hand, I felt like I was floating on air! I felt like every woman in the place envied me because my husband wanted to be with me.
>
> I love to be seen with you. You're so good-looking, and it makes me so proud to have you by my side. Besides, no strange man has ever tried to pick me up when I've been with you!

Can you feel what it would do to your husband to hear your explanation? Suddenly, he would no longer view a trip to the mall as an utter waste of time. In fact, he wouldn't view it as "shopping" at all. The time you took to reveal the reasons behind your need would have completely changed his perspective. Because he is your lover, he would now be motivated by the satisfaction of knowing he was meeting your need. Lovers can't resist that stuff! We're always looking for ways to do that for each other.

There is another benefit as well. By taking the time to show him that your shopping request really is a need, you have gained an enthusiastic escort. That is light-years better than to have some sad old thing tagging along after you with his long face, and who wants to plop down on the nearest bench and wait for you outside every store.

Every Time a Problem Arises, Write It Down

9

O nce you have chosen your hour, start preparing for it. Every time during the week that your spouse does or says something that upsets you, write it down—but don't bring it up. Not yet. Save it for your one-hour appointment.

"Are you saying I should nurse my hard feelings for days at a time until our appointment arrives?"

Absolutely not! As soon as you write down the thing that upset you, immediately get rid of your anger—all of it. Never carry even a portion of your anger over into another day.[1] That's how bitterness worms its way into your heart.[2]

Recording and scheduling the incident to be dealt with later provides a relief valve for your anger. By committing your problem to paper, you are doing something constructive about it. You are not ignoring it, denying it, or hoping it will go away. And because you have a standing one-hour appointment coming up this week, you already know your problem is going to be addressed at the best possible time, in the best possible way.

"But what about the Scripture that says you should go directly to the person the moment you become angry with him?"

The Scripture to which you are probably referring occurs during Jesus' famous Sermon on the Mount:

> Therefore, if you are offering your gift at
> the altar and there remember that your
> brother has something against you, leave your
> gift there in front of the altar. First go and be
> reconciled to your brother; then come and
> offer your gift.[3]

"Yes, that's the one!"

But notice carefully the circumstance under which you are to immediately drop everything and go to your brother. It is not when you first learn of the problem, as a surface reading of this passage might cause you to suppose. It is when you are going about your normal worship and suddenly "remember" your brother's upset. In other words, this is an issue that you knew about before and have let slide. Probably you've procrastinated because you didn't relish the idea of the confrontation!

Jesus is saying, "Your priorities are wrong. I don't want you to sweep this problem under the rug and pretend it isn't there. I value healed relationships among My children more highly than I value material gifts. You've put this off long enough. Now go to him and make it right!"

By setting and keeping your weekly appointment, you are obeying Jesus' intent precisely. In fact, you have assured that every seven days, come rain or shine, whether you are in the mood or not, even though you may not particularly relish the idea of confronting each other, you are going to have to discuss the problems that have arisen between you. That is just the opposite of letting things slide!

There is another qualification many people overlook when they read this part of Jesus' sermon, however. Jesus did not command that you drop everything and immediately go to your brother every time you become angry with him. Instead, this extreme action is to be reserved for those instances when you suddenly remember that you have not yet done anything about the fact that you know your brother has something against you!

There is quite a bit of difference between the two, isn't there? It is not you, the accuser, who shows up on your brother's doorstep uninvited to give your brother a piece of your mind. Instead it is you, the accused, who must humbly present yourself to your brother, because your brother believes you have wronged him and is beginning to wonder if you are ever going to get around to delivering your overdue apology! Once you get a feel for the actual situation Jesus is addressing, the urgency He attaches to it begins to make a lot more sense, doesn't it? (Please refer to the Doorway 29, "Lest You Misunderstand," for a more detailed discussion of how to obey Jesus' teaching when you discover that your spouse is upset with you.)

"But isn't there a Scripture that tells you to immediately go to a person when you are the offended party?"

Almost. The passage to which you refer is Matthew 18:15: Jesus told His disciples,

> If your brother sins against you, go and show him his fault, just between the two of you. If he listens to you, you have won your brother over.

"There you have it!"

Yes, Jesus does tell us to go to the person who has wronged us. Justice demands it. Furthermore, the person may have no idea he has wronged you. When you show him that he has, it gives him the opportunity to apologize and to grow from the experience. Hopefully, it reduces the likelihood that he will do it again—or at least not quite so often as in the past!

But nowhere in this passage does Jesus tell you that you must drop everything you are doing and demand an immediate audience with the person who has wronged you. Ninety-nine times out of a hundred, your standing weekly appointment is plenty soon enough.

At first glance, "having it out" with your spouse the moment a problem arises sounds wise. But in everyday life situations, it seldom works. First, that is when your emotions are hardest to control. The hurt is fresh, it stings and, as a result, so do your words. Consequently, you end up saying things to each other you don't really mean. And that makes matters worse than they were to begin with.

By waiting, you both get a chance to cool off. Once the fire has died down, you are much more likely to choose your words lovingly and with care.

Suppose your husband is late five times this week. On this, the fifth time, he has forgotten that you needed the car for your dentist appointment. Even before he finishes stammering out his lame excuse, you interrupt with, "You have got to be the most self-centered, inconsiderate man on earth!"

He tries to tell you he is sorry, but his apology falls on deaf ears. Gathering steam, you get straight to the bottom line. "You say you love me, but you couldn't. Because if you did, you would have done whatever you had to do to be here on time!"

Brilliant move. Because he made you miss your fluoride treatment, you have now ensured that you will both eat dinner in silence, that the entire evening will be spent with the tension so thick you could cut it with a knife, and that the hours between 10:30 P.M. and 6:00 A.M. will be spent in bed back-to-back, with each of you going to great lengths not to so much as touch a tiny toe of the other. You've managed to turn a minor border incident into World War III! That's quite a diplomatic feat.

If you are used to confronting each other whenever your problems occur, that scenario sounds more than a little familiar. Why in the world would you deliberately choose to do that to the most precious relationship you have on the face of the earth?

By challenging your husband over his lateness each time, you have delivered five roundhouse blows to the chin of your marriage. How many more of those hard punches do you think your marriage can withstand before it topples, glassy-eyed, to the canvas? Why have five spur-of-the-moment, totally ineffective, emotional blowouts, when only one calm, carefully thought-out discussion is much more likely to succeed?

The delayed approach works better because it gives you time to consider the possibility that there might be a root cause to your recurring problem. When keeping track of their irritations for a week, most couples are surprised to learn that they really don't have that many different problems. In most cases they just keep having the same few over and over again!

As you review your notes prior to your one-hour meeting, that pattern will begin to emerge. During your time together, then, you will both be much better equipped to brainstorm until you track down the difficulty that is actually causing your pain.

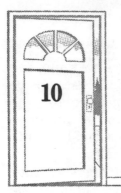

10

Take Care of First Things First

You're telling me that there are times when I may have to wait nearly a week before we even attempt to resolve our problem! Isn't that like allowing an open wound to go untreated for days?"

Good analogy. The answer is "Absolutely not." Your once-a-week appointment will enable you to close the wound faster than you have ever closed it before.

One day when I was seven years old, I ran over to where a friend of our family was trying to start our Wizard power lawn mower. A notoriously cold starter, the old mower was being cantankerous again that day. As the exhausted man pulled the rope again and again, he failed to notice that I had knelt down on the grass too close to the mower.

Finally, he took hold of the rope with both hands and jerked with all his might. The old mower's front wheels leaped up into the air at a crazy angle, the engine suddenly roared to life, and the furiously spinning blade came down on top of my bent left knee.

Instinctively, my hands flew to clutch my left thigh above the knee in a terrified death grip. Blood was everywhere. As the mower was lifted off my knee, I looked with horror into the gaping hole the blade had ripped out of my leg, and saw exposed the grisly white of my own left femur.

Thinking quickly, the man grabbed the lawn mower rope, hastily wrapped it around my left thigh, and jerked it into a tight tourniquet. A crowd quickly gathered, and my dad came running up to learn what had happened. I saw the man shake his head and heard him whisper to my dad not quite softly enough, "I'm afraid he's going to lose the leg." It was then that I began to cry.

They raced me to the hospital emergency room where Doctor Everett Mason feverishly worked for hours to save my leg. I cannot begin to describe the relief that swept over me when they told me he had succeeded. I would walk again, run again, play football again. A jagged scar over my knee would be the only reminder of the day when I came within a quarter inch of losing my left leg.

That is what happened. But please take special note of what did *not* happen. I did not grab my leg and scream out, "Arrest this man! He just butchered my leg with a power mower!"

Our family friend did not call my dad over and demand, "Dick, your son came over here and deliberately knelt too close to the mower while I was trying to start it. I'm sure you've told him to stay away from power equipment. I think he deserves a good spanking!"

Nor did my father grab the man by his lapels and shake him until his teeth rattled, while yelling, "You irresponsible fool! Why in the world did you keep trying to start that mower with a child kneeling right next to it?"

There was plenty of time for sorting through what happened and coming up with a plan for preventing its recurrence later. What mattered the most in those crucial hours immediately after the accident was saving my leg.

Do you get the message? When a gaping wound is

suddenly ripped open in your marriage, the last thing you need is an immediate confrontation over who did what to whom. Your first priority is to close the wound—not to tear into each other and rip it open even wider.

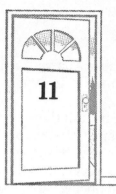

Here's How to Close Your Wound

11

S tart with a "tourniquet." Staunch the flow of "blood" by refusing to dwell on your hurt or your anger. If you allow the "How *could* he's?" and the "How *dare* she's?" to continue to flow, you will be emotionally weakened and may even go into shock. You simply cannot allow yourself to fret, fume, and stew over what your mate did or failed to do. You need your wits about you and all the strength you can muster in order to concentrate on damage control. You've lost enough "blood" already. So stop it—right now.

Next, get to the "hospital" as quickly as possible, and ask your "doctor" to start operating. Get alone in your car, retire to a room where you can have some privacy, or go for a walk...and turn your case over to God. Tell Him what happened. Pour out your feelings. Describe for Him how angry your spouse has made you, or how deeply you are hurt. Get rid of it—absolutely all of it. And then ask Him to perform spiritual surgery on your open wound.

Let me give you some reassurance right here. God has never yet lost a "leg" or a "patient." He is the Great Physician. He knows your psyche, your personal needs, and your emotional makeup better than anyone, as only your Creator can. The "surgery" God performs on you will always be a success. You will be able to walk, to run, to laugh, and to love again.

Finally, return as often as needed for "physical therapy." Every time you start to get a little "stiff" emotionally, open God's "exercise manual" (the Bible) and follow the instructions inside. If you stick to your recovery program religiously, you will not only regain full use of your "leg," but the "exercises" you perform will actually make you stronger than you were before your "injury."

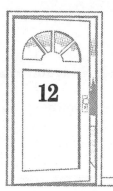

"But How Do You Keep Your Spouse From Walking All Over You?"

12

A ll right," I can just hear you saying at this point, "I can see how my husband and I are both going to enjoy 167 out of 168 argument-free hours every week. I can even see the wisdom of handling our problems so that we are sharing needs, rather than complaints. But what happens if my husband decides to take advantage of this gentle approach, and ignores all my 'shared needs' in a particular area?"

Good question. First, let me remind you that this book is *For Lovers Only*—and that this is one of the biggest reasons why. Couples who have still not settled the basic issues of integrity, openness, and honesty in their marriages may be ill-advised to attempt this approach. They have so much to deal with and so many serious issues to wrestle to the ground that they may well have to take an entirely different approach until, with God's help, they are able to nurse their marriages out of intensive care.

By contrast, you are lovers. By very definition, you are givers, not takers. Therefore, the approach we are recommending is much safer for you.

"Are you saying that lovers *never* take advantage of each other?"

No. Lovers are not perfect. Even lovers have their bad days, their low times, their periods of spiritual sickness. It is entirely possible that on one or more occasions through the years you will enter a temporary, but nevertheless "dark" phase of your marriage, when your spouse ceases to behave like a lover.

"So what do I do, if that should ever occur?"

If your spouse continues to keep the one-hour appointment with you, be persistent about presenting your concerns as needs, rather than complaints. But if, after a significant time has gone by, you become completely convinced that your spouse is making absolutely no attempt to correct the offensive behavior, then you are left with no alternative. You must become directive.

Jesus modeled this behavior when He lashed out at the Pharisees:

> Woe to you, teachers of the law and Pharisees, you hypocrites! You travel over land and sea to win a single convert, and when he becomes one, you make him twice as much a son of hell as you are.
>
> Woe to you, teachers of the law and Pharisees, you hypocrites! You are like whitewashed tombs, which look beautiful on the outside but on the inside are full of dead men's bones and everything unclean. In the same way, on the outside you appear to people as righteous but on the inside you are full of hypocrisy and wickedness.
>
> You snakes! You brood of vipers! How will you escape being condemned to hell?[1]

The operative word, here, is "hypocrite." Jesus flayed these religious leaders alive because they were making no attempt whatsoever to live up to the high religious standards they preached. Their religion was all pretense.

Contrast His language here, however, with the gentle way He handled the woman taken in the very act of adultery: "Then neither do I condemn you.... Go now and leave your life of sin."[2]

In spite of His hatred for sin, God deals tenderly with the weak sinner:

> The Lord is compassionate and gracious,
>   slow to anger, abounding in love.
> He will not always accuse,
>   nor will he harbor his anger forever;
> he does not treat us as our sins deserve
>   or repay us according to our iniquities.
> For he knows how we are formed,
>   he remembers that we are dust.[3]

So it is not sin, per se, that deserves to be lambasted. It is hypocrisy. It is the refusal to even attempt to do what is right. The spouse who has sunk to that low state is dull and hardened. He or she is no longer spiritually sensitive enough to respond to a tenderly worded request to meet your needs.

Love demands, therefore, that should this sad condition ever befall your mate, you must intervene with language that is sufficiently directive to penetrate the barrier that has been erected.

Please remember, however, that this is an extreme measure, to be used only when you have no alternative. Do not allow impatience or residual anger to goad you into a premature outburst. You will live to regret it.

As long as you see the slightest effort to do right on your spouse's part, continue to share your needs, and double your prayers. Remember that at this point you are engaged in a spiritual battle. In spite of the temptation to do so, you dare not weaken your position by losing your temper and sinning against your mate.

If you both remain faithful to your weekly sessions, problems of a truly severe magnitude will seldom develop. Most of the difficulties in marriage begin as a pesky fly that won't go away. Most of the time, your weekly appointment is more than sufficient to resolve those issues before they escalate into something bigger. Why use an atomic bomb when a fly swatter will do... unless you really enjoy the fallout.

13 *You Do Not Need an Apology From Your Spouse!*

=====//=====

I wouldn't blame you one bit if you are now saying to yourself, "But I don't see how I can get rid of my hurt or my anger all by myself. Don't I have to receive an apology from my spouse before I can completely get over it?

The answer is "No, you do not." Apologies are essential to give but nonessential to receive. If you know that you owe your spouse an apology (or anyone else for that matter), you have no choice but to give it. To do any less will cause erosion in your character.

It does not work both ways, however. Even when you are certain that your spouse owes you an apology, you can nevertheless learn to live a happy, successful life without ever receiving the apology you believe you are owed.

There are several very good reasons why this is true. First, you may be mistaken. Even though you sincerely believe that your husband has wronged you, he may not, in fact, owe you an apology. Secondly, your wife may indeed have wronged you, but she honestly may not be able to see that she has. In that case, she cannot truthfully apologize for something that she cannot grasp that she has done. Finally, your husband may owe it and know it but refuse to show it. To complicate matters even further, sometimes it is extremely difficult to be able to tell which of the three is the real reason why you are not receiving the apology you desire.

No matter which is the case, however, they all have one infuriating thing in common: You ain't gonna get an apology! You are absolutely helpless. Which brings up a compelling question: What kind of God would make your emotional recovery contingent upon the apology of another person over whose behavior you have absolutely no control?

But He didn't do that to you. Instead, He has granted you the right to call upon Him to achieve emotional well-being, with or without the cooperation of your spouse.

So don't get the two mixed up. Your mechanism for recovering from hurt or anger is totally *separate* from your spouse's decision to ask your forgiveness. Perhaps it will help you to see the two as independent functions if you step back a bit and consider a parallel incident outside of the marital/emotional spectrum.

Suppose a drunk driver ran a traffic light and smashed into your car, breaking your left arm. Would your arm be able to heal, even if the drunk never sent you a note telling you he was sorry? Certainly. God has built into your system the capacity for self-repair. On the other hand, if the drunk driver called you daily, begging for forgiveness, would that cause the doctor to take your arm out of the cast even one day sooner? Probably not.

And so it is with your damaged emotions. One of the more obvious proofs of this simple truth is that not everyone gets angry or hurt over the same things you do. You may become furious with your husband when he tromps through the house with his muddy boots right after you cleaned the floors. But believe it or not, there are some wives out there who don't allow that to upset them at all.

If you really wanted to, you could train yourself to do as they do. You could learn to stay calm, to give your hard-working man an affectionate hello kiss, and then to add with a twinkle in your eye, "Darling, when you get a chance this evening, would you please clean up the mud that fell off your boots when you came in?"

"That would never work for me!" you may sputter. "For one thing, my husband wouldn't clean the floors properly. He'd take a couple of swipes at it, leaving hunks of mud everywhere, and then expect me to praise him the rest of the evening for going above and beyond the call of duty!"

Okay, okay. Then let's not compare you with someone else. Let's just compare you with *you*. Why don't we talk to your husband now to enable you to see in him what you may have difficulty seeing in yourself.

Have you ever noticed, Sir, that your anger is not uniform? Monday night you got all misty-eyed when you saw your little boy's toys in the driveway, choked up over how fortunate you were to be a daddy. The very next day when you drove up and saw those same toys in the driveway, you flew off the handle and stormed into the house complaining, "Why is it that every time I come home I have to stop, get out, and move a dozen pieces of junk before I can put my car in the garage?"

"I can explain that," you say. "Monday morning's newspaper carried a story about a little boy who died of leukemia. I was so grateful just to have my kids alive that the toys didn't bother me that day. In fact, when I saw them scattered everywhere in the driveway, I told myself, 'I'll bet that the parents of that little boy who had leukemia would give anything to see some toys in their driveway today.'"

"Tuesday, though, was another story. That morning the computer was down and I lost half a day's productivity.

Then that afternoon an account we had serviced for five years called to say they were switching their business to a competitor. By the time I got home, I was in no mood to have to deal with a bunch of toys blocking my path."

I understand, of course. We've all been there. But that's just the point. Your anger had nothing to do with your kids or with their toys in the driveway. For that matter, it wasn't even what you had read in the paper on Monday morning, the computer failure, or the account that flew the coup.

It was your own very personal reaction to each of those events that determined your decision to become angry—not the events themselves, and not the people involved in each of those events. It was your mood, your response—you, just you.

"I've tried. Honestly I have. But I simply cannot get rid of my anger until I've talked it out with my spouse!"

Of course you can. In fact, if you don't want your discussion to make things even worse, you had *better* get rid of your anger before you launch your discussion!

"Well, I don't see how. Maybe I'm just different. All I really know is that my particular personality is such that I *have* to hear an apology before I can let go of my anger."

No, you don't. What are you going to do on those occasions when your spouse honestly doesn't think she owes you an apology? Refuse to forgive her? As we have already seen, that is simply not an option for the obedient Christian. Jesus told His disciples,

> If you forgive men when they sin against
> you, your heavenly Father will also forgive
> you. But if you do not forgive men their sins,
> your Father will not forgive your sins."[1]

Jesus not only taught that to His disciples, but He practiced what He preached. Who would be one of the hardest people in the world to forgive? How about your murderer—while he was in the very act of murdering you? And yet, that is exactly what Jesus did while He hung on the cross. "Father, forgive them," Jesus said, "for they do not know what they are doing."[2]

Did Jesus mean that they were unaware they were crucifying Him? Of course not. They were knowingly and deliberately putting Him to death. What He meant was that they had justified their murderous behavior.

Did any of them come up to Him and apologize for what they were doing? On the contrary, they mocked Him, sneered at Him, and hurled insults at Him.[3]

"But I've never before been able to get over something without first hashing it out!"

It *is* difficult! But this is what maturing in Christ is all about. Of *course* it is hard! But it is not something of which you are incapable. God never issues an impossible command. Instead, if you really beg Him for His help, you will find that His strength will provide you with the ability to forgive... even before you obtain your longed-for apology!

In fact, there is another reason why it is extremely important that you learn to totally separate forgiveness from apology. Even if you knew you could extract an apology from your spouse every single time, you would still be making a serious mistake to withhold your forgiveness until you received your spouse's apology. In that case, all you would really be saying is, "I'll forgive you—but only after I get my way!" And that is a long, long distance from the humble, Christlike spirit that makes for great marriages and healthy Christians.

"This sounds like you are putting all the responsibility on me! Doesn't my spouse share some of the blame, as well?"

Certainly, your spouse is totally responsible for his or her own actions. But only you are responsible for your reaction to your spouse's actions! The up-side to all of this is the liberating knowledge that since you and only you are responsible for your emotional state, nobody else has the right—or even the ability, unless you grant it to them—to prevent you from enjoying full emotional health.

No matter how intolerant your wife may appear to be Wednesday afternoon, no matter how inconsiderately your husband may come across when he forgets the anniversary of the day he asked you to marry him, your spouse cannot *make* you become hurt or angry. But if and when you do become angry, you and you alone have the power to halt the emotional damage whenever you decide that is what you want to do—with or without the cooperation of your spouse.

The Easiest Time to Recover Emotionally Is Before Discussion!

14

Many times you are not, in fact, getting rid of your anger or your hurt when you discuss the problem with your spouse immediately. All too often you leave your emotions still simmering because most discussions treat the symptoms rather than the cause. Although you may have negotiated a settlement with your spouse that involved mutual compromise, that in no way guarantees that you appropriately addressed the hurt or the anger you felt.

By contrast, when you save your discussion until later, an interesting thing occurs: Your hurt is isolated. Since you cannot spar with your spouse, you are left with nothing but your anger to deal with, and you are much more likely to see it for exactly what it is.

As we have already seen, it is unpleasant to recognize, certainly. You would probably prefer to dump the responsibility for your emotional distress at your spouse's feet. But the truth is, you are the only one who can rid yourself of your own destructive emotions. Your husband cannot do it for you even if he apologizes for the next eight hours, down on his knees—attractive as that thought may be! Your wife cannot do it for you, even if she decides to cave in and totally let you have your own way—though you tell yourself it would be so nice to experience, just this once!

Instead, waiting to discuss it with your spouse until the arrival of your next one-hour appointment forces you to face reality. If you are going to experience any relief before then, you are going to have to take matters into your own hands. And that is precisely the pair of hands in which the responsibility for your emotional recovery belongs.

15 When Do You Call an Emergency Session?

S o is that it? Are there no exceptions, even in case of an emergency?"

Of course you can make an exception. You may be aware of a scheduled event that is coming up before your appointment and know that if the two of you don't talk beforehand, the result will be absolutely intolerable. In that case, use common sense.

For example, your husband may be given to making loud, disparaging comments about modern art. As an art major in college, you may find his reactions uninformed and offensive. You've been meaning to bring it up in your one-hour meetings, but until now other items have had higher priority.

Now, however, your husband has just called to say that his boss has invited the two of you to accompany him and his wife to an art show at the museum tomorrow night. You happen to know that the entire exhibit is devoted to modern art! To complicate matters, your weekly need-sharing appointment with your husband isn't until Saturday afternoon. So what do you do: refuse to say anything and let him make a fool of himself in front of his boss tomorrow night? Of course not.

Call your husband back and say to him, "Guess what? That show we're going to at the museum tomorrow night is devoted exclusively to modern art!" Wait for his groan and then say, "Tell you what—I'd like to call a special emergency session on this subject, for tonight after supper. What do you say?"

There are three things to keep in mind when you have to resort to an emergency session. First, deal with the emergency issue only. Resist the temptation to tackle your other problems at the same time, "since we're already having a meeting." It may sound more efficient to switch your entire weekly one-hour appointment to the emergency time, but in practice it seldom works. For one thing, neither of you has had enough time to properly prepare for the entire meeting, and it is your advance, thoughtful preparation that ensures the success of each session. But there is another consideration, as well.

If you cancel your regular appointment time this week, there is an increased danger that you will find another "good" reason to cancel it next week. That will throw off your entire weekly rhythm, make it impossible for either of you to reliably schedule your advance preparation time, and will therefore greatly reduce the effectiveness of your meetings. You have to treat your weekly appointment time as almost "sacred" or the vicious crush of your busy schedules will quickly swallow it up.

Secondly, be sure to observe the normal need-sharing guidelines during your emergency session. Don't throw out all the principles you've learned about communicating with your lover and in the name of haste "just get down to brass tacks." In ten minutes that approach can set your relationship back six months!

Finally, keep your emergency appointments rare. It is all too easy to slip into a crisis mentality that demands to deal with this issue now "because I am thinking about it now." Please think twice before you do—and then think again. There are very, very, *very* few issues that cannot wait to be discussed at your weekly, predetermined time.

16

Do Your Homework Before Your Meeting

———— # ————

Once your emotional wound has been closed and has started to heal, it is time for you to give the entire incident the attention it deserves. You may want to write down exactly what happened, step-by-step. If this is a recurring problem, you might find it helpful to plot out the time, frequency, and relative severity of each incident on a sheet of graph paper. If you wish, you can go to the library and research the problem, in the case of difficulties that occur with enough frequency to have been written up in reliable books and magazines. You may even want to enter all the factors into your computer and analyze them backward and forward.

Why? Because you don't want to keep facing this same problem again and again, week after week, month after month, and year after year. That's why!

"But don't I need my spouse's input in this process?"

Yes you do. But it is so much more productive if you have first paid the price to really think it through, to walk all around the situation, and to view it from every conceivable angle. The more emotional your makeup, the more important it is for you to do this first. Otherwise, you can end up

66

discussing irrelevant issues and using your precious time to work on symptoms rather than on their underlying causes.

Certainly, you need to discuss it with your spouse during your weekly meeting. But it is always wise to do your homework *before* you sit for your final exam. In this case, there is a lot more at stake than an "A" on your report card!

Furthermore, whatever you do, don't show up for your hour ill-prepared, distracted, or without your notes. Your spouse will feel devalued and defeated. If you like the idea of keeping all your quarrels confined to a single hour each week, then you are going to have to pay the price and make that hour really count when it arrives.

You'll Be Glad You Did Your Homework!

S uppose your husband has been grouchy with you lately. Why not just confront him on the spot and tell him to knock it off? What is there to analyze about someone who is being a grouch? Why not tell him, "Hey, guy—get over it! I'm a human being, and I expect to be treated like one!"?

"Oh, no!" you say. "You've convinced me of the dangers of taking cheap shots on the spot and ruining our whole day. I'm willing to wait until our weekly meeting and express it as a need. But I certainly don't need to give any advance thought to it. It's a simple matter of reminding him to be courteous, that's all."

And how will you bring it up?

"All right, I see your point. Obviously, I will have to give it a tiny bit of thought. Let's see—I'll just tell him, 'Sweetheart, I really need you to be kind to me at all times.' That should take care of it. After all, it's not that big a deal."

Are you sure?

"Am I sure of what?"

Are you sure "it's not that big a deal"?

"Of course I'm sure. I mean, what else could it be?"

That's just the point. Until you analyze it, you can't be sure it's not that big a deal. People don't normally change their behavior without a reason, you know.

"Okay, I'll buy that. But where in the world do I start?"

First of all, you might ask yourself if he is grouchy all the time or primarily during one period of the day.

"Well, now that you mention it, it's almost always in the evenings."

Precisely when in the evenings?

"I'm not sure."

Then you need to be an observer for several nights. (Let's suppose you have now completed your fieldwork.) You've had a chance to observe your husband for several days now. When in the evenings does he start getting grouchy?

"At 9:00 P.M.! It's almost like a shade is pulled over his eyes at that time, and he literally undergoes a personality change!"

Does anything in particular bring it on?

"No, that's just it! We can be sitting together in the living room talking when suddenly he becomes very irritable with me for absolutely no reason. Or maybe we will be reading quietly when all at once he will throw down the newspaper as though he is angry about something!"

So, what does he do after that?

"Well, it just gets worse. He withdraws into his shell, refuses to communicate beyond a few grunts, and then the next thing I know, he's gone to bed—sometimes without even saying good night!"

What time would you say he ends up going to bed?

"Oh, maybe 9:30 or 10:00."

Is that his normal bedtime?

"No, he hates to go to bed before 11:00. Evenings have always been his favorite time to relax and unwind. He likes to stretch them out as long as he can."

Is he getting enough sleep?

"No, he's not, but it's his own fault. He's been setting his alarm for 4:30 A.M., and going in to the office early every morning."

How long ago did he start getting up this early?

"I'm not sure. Maybe two weeks."

And how long ago did he start getting grouchy at 9:00 in the evenings?

"About...two weeks ago!"

Quite a coincidence.

"So that's it? He's grouchy just because he's short on sleep?"

I don't know. What do you think?

"Well, that's got to be at least part of the answer. Come to think of it, he always has been a little crabby when he falls behind on his eight hours a night."

As crabby as he has been the last two weeks?

"Well, no. It's been worse this time."

Then, let's try to determine what else is going on. Why is your husband going in to the office so early?

"He says he's working against a deadline for a major customer."

So is he enjoying his work on this project?

"No. He really resents it. He thinks his boss is trying to get promoted to vice president by driving him unmercifully—giving him more work than any two normal men should be asked to do."

Hmmmm. Tell me something about *how* your husband gets grouchy in the evening. Is it ever directed specifically at you?

"Well, I'm right there in the room, and it's very unpleasant!"

Yes, but when he gets grouchy, does he criticize you for something you have done, or tell you that he is unhappy with you personally?

"Well, now that you mention it, no."

So, who do you think his anger is really directed at?

"It must be...his boss!"

Why doesn't he just tell his boss how he feels?

"He's afraid to! He's only been with this company six months, and he has since learned that his boss has a reputation for firing employees when they cross him."

Why doesn't he look for work elsewhere?

"Because, in spite of the boss he has right now, this is a really good company. He's wanted to work there for years, and just now got his chance. Besides, it wouldn't look good on his resumé if he changed jobs every six months."

So, Sherlock Holmes, what's your assessment of the situation so far?

"Okay, to begin with I would say that my husband starts feeling groggy at 9:00 every night because he is short on sleep."

And?

"He probably feels cheated about having the rest of his evening ruined because he can hardly keep his eyes open."

And?

"He's probably already thinking about that alarm that's going to go off in the middle of the night, having breakfast alone, and leaving the house for work while it's still dark."

You're doing very well! Keep going.

"It could be that when he pulls into his shell, he's starting to feel pressured about all the work he has to do when he arrives at the office."

Reasonable guess—what else?

"You know, he probably feels totally boxed in. He's being treated unfairly, and its affecting him physically and emotionally—but he can't say a word about it, for fear of getting fired. On top of everything, it has to be very disillusioning to him to finally get a position with the company he has always wanted to work for and to discover that he enjoys it less than anywhere else he has ever worked!"

Excellent. Are you ready to bring this up in your next weekly session, now?

"Yes, I think I am. No, wait a minute! The truth is, his grouchiness doesn't have a thing to do with me. He just feels trapped, and doesn't know how to get out. What he really needs is my support."

Now, you're cooking. How are you going to give it to him?

"That will take a little more planning—good grief! I had no idea how complicated a little evening grouchiness could actually turn out to be!"

Exactly.

"But I know one thing I can do right away."

What's that?

"Tonight at about 8:45 I'm going to tell him to come over to the couch and put his head in my lap."

Do you think he'll cooperate?

"Sure! It's before 9:00 P.M., remember? Besides, he loves to lay his head in my lap and let me run my fingers through his hair. That's how I help him get rid of his headaches. He says it soothes and relaxes him."

Good move. Then what?

"Then I'll ask him to tell me what he's thinking. I'll ask him how it's going at work, how he's getting along with his boss, things like that."

And?

"I'll let him know that I understand what he's going through, that I want him to keep giving me daily updates so I will be able to understand what he's facing, and that I will always be there for him, because I really believe in him."

Not bad! How do you think he will respond?

"When I talk to him like that, he always gets all tender and lovey-dovey toward me."

I see.

"Wait a minute, I'm not finished. So then, instead of letting him go to bed alone, I think I'll go to bed with him—although I can't guarantee that we'll go right to sleep!"

Well done! It sounds as though you are going to be able to manage things quite nicely from here on out.

"Is This the Time to Address Our Sexual Problems?"

18

A bsolutely. If there was ever a subject that needed to be brought up as a need rather than a complaint, this is it!

You have already discovered the hard way that one tiny mistake in this area can set your love life back for a long, long time. Because you are lovers, your ability to satisfy each other sexually is a source of real pride to you. It can be devastating to your mate to discover that you don't think he's as good in bed as he thought he was!

So really do your homework for this one. The general rule here is, the more sensitive the issue, the more time is needed for advance preparation. It would be better to put off discussing it for a week, or even two, than to rush right in and pour cold water all over your mate's sexual responsiveness because you haven't given the matter sufficient thought.

As always, when you prepare you should approach the subject from your spouse's point of view. But it is doubly important to do so when the subject is sex. If your spouse has been disinterested in sex lately, the last thing you want to barge in with is, "I need more sex!" Instead, explore all the things going on in your spouse's life that could be siphoning off the significant energy required for a strong libido.

If on the other hand you want to try something new but you have detected a little reluctance on your spouse's part, be sure to ask yourself why. Most lovers are game for anything, so long as they feel secure. What is there about your request that may be touching an area of insecurity? Does it involve a part of your wife's body that she doesn't feel good about? Is it possible that your husband may be uncertain that he can perform exactly as you expect?

Without realizing it, your request may be reminding your spouse of a past bad experience. Can you remember a time when the two of you tried something similar and it flopped? Or it may have nothing to do with you. Think back to the discussions you have had with your spouse about past relationships with other people: parents, dates, even former spouses. Was there anything you can remember that may be coming back to haunt your spouse now? Or it may be that your request violates a prohibition that your spouse has read about or heard from someone else.

Of course, even though you draw a blank on some of these possibilities, that does not necessarily mean that they do not apply. It may simply be that you and your spouse have never got around to discussing them yet. Therefore, you will want to list them in your preparatory notes for your one-hour session, bring them with you, and use them when and if the discussion warrants it.

"Delicacy"—that is your watchword. No matter how familiar the two of you have become sexually, it is nevertheless essential that you handle sexual complaints or unmet sexual desires almost as though you and your spouse were about to go to bed together for the first time.

Take nothing for granted. Never be coarse or crude. The moment your wife becomes aware that you are addressing her sexual performance in this meeting, her sensitivity will suddenly magnify a hundredfold. Handle her tender sensibilities with a deep respect that approaches reverence.

One more thing. It is always wise to reassure your spouse before, during, and after you address one of your sexual needs. You have to remember that the first question that will pop into your husband's mind when it dawns on him that you're on the subject of sex is, "Am I an inadequate sexual partner?" You need to plan in advance exactly how you will alleviate his fears, or you could make matters worse rather than better. Specific examples of how to accomplish this are included in Secret Number Two, "Make Love in the Garden of Eden."

How to Respond to a Request You Don't Understand

To this point we've spent most of our time talking about how to get your needs across to your mate. Now let's take a closer look at how you want to respond when your spouse shares one of her needs with you.

Suppose she says, "Honey, I need you to show me that you love me."

You might be tempted to answer, "Okay, Doll, I'll really try," and then hurry to the next item on your agenda.

But don't do that. Your objective in this hour is not to cover as many different subjects as you can, but to thoroughly understand each need before you bring up the next topic. There's a reason she asked you to show her that you love her. Your mission is to discover that underlying need and take a crash course in exactly how to meet it.

Every time your spouse makes such a request, regard it as a flashing signal that there is something important about her that you had better learn. She probably thinks it is all very obvious—and to her it is. But it probably isn't at all clear to you. In fact, chances are excellent that you don't even know what subject she's on! Think about it. If you already understood what she was talking about, she probably wouldn't have had to bring it up in the first place!

This will become immediately apparent when you ask her a couple of follow-up questions. So start asking:

"Okay, Sweetheart, how can I show you that I love you?"

"Well, you know—" she may reply, still thinking that her request is obvious. "By what you say and do."

Since you can swap general statements like this all day long, it's time to embark on a fishing expedition. Give her an example or two of what you think she means by her request. You will probably be wrong, but at least you'll have begun to narrow down the field.

"You mean like telling you I love you or calling you during the day when I get a break?"

"Well, yes," she may answer, frowning slightly, "but not exactly."

Don't be impatient at this point. She isn't deliberately avoiding your question. It's just that she still doesn't realize the magnitude of your communication gap. But since you are starting to catch on to just how big that gap indeed may be, keep pressing on!

Ask, "Is there something I can improve about the way I tell you that I love you?"

She may respond, "Well, of course I like to hear you say the words, 'I love you,' but I need to hear more."

"Such as?"

"Such as how much do you love me?"

Be careful here. As a male, you are likely to regard her request as facetious and be tempted to respond with a made-up concrete quantity to show her how ridiculous it is. But resist the urge to pop off with some crack like, "Oh, now I understand! Hey, no problem! I love you exactly four million, three hundred fifty-three thousand, two hundred seventy-eight dollars and ninety-two cents' worth. Anything else you want to know?"

One smart-aleck statement like that, and you may as well forget the sexual request you were going to make as your grand finale for the hour! She is dead serious. She honestly wants you to tell her how much you love her. It's time to admit that you're stumped.

"Baby, I love you more than life itself, but I don't know how to tell you how much that is. Can you help me better understand what you mean?"

"Not bad!" she may respond with a smile.

"What do you mean, 'Not bad!'?"

"You just told me you love me more than life itself! Now that's a lot!"

"You mean that's it? I did it? That's what you want to hear when you ask how much I love you?"

"Umm-hmmmm."

A 15-watt bulb will click on high among the hanging bats somewhere in the dark cavern of your male mind. "So what you want to hear is comparisons! You want to hear me say, 'I love you more than I ever dreamed possible'... I love you so much it sometimes brings tears to my eyes.'

"You want me to tell you, 'When we were first married, I thought I loved you as much as it was possible for a man to love a woman. But compared to how much I love you now, I realize that back then I didn't even understand the meaning of the word "love."' So that's what you want me to say!"

Watch her. She'll be searching your eyes when she replies, "Only if that's how much you really do love me."

"I do, Darling," you can reassure her, "with all my heart I do. Thank you for helping me understand what you need from me."

It's liberating, isn't it? Now you know how to communicate your love to your wife in a way that hits home. The next time you call her from work, you can have one ready: "I love you today more than I loved you yesterday...but not nearly as much as I'll love you tomorrow."

Just be sure you use a private line when you ring out. Any male who picks up the phone and accidentally overhears your love talk may be overcome with an acute case of nausea. On the other hand, any woman listening in probably will turn green with envy!

Don't Get Defensive!

Suppose your husband says as tactfully as he knows how, "You know, once our children have moved out, I hope with all my heart that God gives us at least another 30 years together, just the two of us. But Baby, that's not going to happen unless we take good care of ourselves. I can't bear the idea of having our future together cut short, like Dad had to go through when he lost Mom.

"For my sake, would you be willing to go back on your diet and stay with it until you reach your goal weight? Honey, I love you just the way you are—honest, I do! But that's not the issue. It's just that I love you too much to lose you!"

Now, he has just made a gallant attempt to turn his complaint into a loving need. In order to spare your feelings, he has skirted the more volatile issues about your excess weight. He deliberately did not mention how much prouder of a slimmer you he would be when the two of you are out together in public. He certainly did not bring up the fact that if you took off those 30 pounds you need to lose, it might do wonders for his flagging sex drive.

Instead, he obviously spent some time thinking it through. He carefully selected the least selfish, most loving, most important reason he could imagine to motivate you to lose weight. But did all his homework do any good? Not much.

What you actually heard him say was, "Hey Fatso! I can't stand the sight of all that blubber!"

Because you already feel so much guilt about being overweight, you are extremely sensitive in this area. Although he touched you there as gently as he knew how, it felt to you like being smacked in the face with a rotten 30-pound tuna!

If you aren't careful, you may be tempted to blow him out of the water with a broadside. "Of all the nerve! You've got a lot of room to talk, you know that? I nibble like a bird while you chow down like a pig, and who puts on the weight? I do! It's just not fair. If you wanted one of those skinny little models like you see on TV, why didn't you just marry one? I can't believe you brought this up. I really can't!"

Or you could say nothing and merely burst into tears. Either way, you'll have destroyed the effectiveness of your hour together.

Do you know what? The truth is, your husband is right. You do need to lose weight. Furthermore, down deep you have known all along that it would please him very much if you took off those extra pounds.

Could he have brought up the subject more delicately? Perhaps. Could he have worded his request more considerately? Maybe so. But behind all your wounded feelings, your hurt, and your anger, lies a single cause: your guilt. Because the truth is that if you were not overweight, he never would have had to bring it up.

"That's just it!" you may be tempted to react. "He didn't *have* to bring it up! He knows how many diets I've been on.

He knows how hard I've tried! Why didn't he just leave well enough alone? Why did he have to heap more guilt on top of all the guilt I already carry?"

I hear you, and I hurt for you because of the ferocious battle you have waged, perhaps since you were a little girl. You probably have a genetic predisposition toward excess weight. You are absolutely right when you point out that some people can eat more than you eat and not gain nearly as much weight. It is entirely possible that your metabolism is slower and less efficient than theirs.

Thin people have absolutely no concept of how hard it is for you to give up eating those things you really enjoy in favor of foods that leave you feeling empty and unsatisfied. They can't even begin to comprehend how hard it is for you to overcome ten, twenty, thirty, or more years of food-dependent behavior overnight. There is a sense in which thin people do not even live in the same world you live in—not even in the same galaxy!

So why *did* your husband bring this up? Why can't he see that you are already doing your best? Whatever happened to unconditional love? Why can't he just accept you as you are? And if, by God's grace, some day you are miraculously able to lose some weight, then why can't he treat it as an unexpected, entirely unnecessary blessing?

Well, this much you know. Your husband is not some inconsiderate lout. He is your lover. And he has lived with you long enough to observe your struggles. Even though he may not be able to fathom the agony you go through, he senses that it must be awesome.

In light of his knowledge, then why *did* he bring it up? Why didn't he just content himself by being thankful for all of your other marvelous attributes and leave your overweight problem untouched? After all, nobody is perfect—including your husband!

Could it be that it really is because he cares? Could it be that he has looked down the corridor of time and has imagined what it would be like to lose you? Could it be that he is so in love with you that he can't bear the thought of having to live without you? Could that be what drove him to bring it up?

Could it even be that the Holy Spirit may have prompted him to say something, in order to provide you with the additional incentive you need to finally defeat this monster that has stalked you all your life? Could it be, in other words, that it wasn't selfishness at all that prompted your husband's words? Could it be that the only thing that enabled him to overcome his extreme reluctance to mention it at all was pure, unadulterated love?

Please trust your spouse's motives. Don't allow guilt-ridden defensiveness to cheat you out of the incalculable benefit of his or her gentle request.

Now summon all your self-control and tell your spouse, "You're right, Honey, I'll do my best."

If you are too affected emotionally and don't trust yourself to speak, just nod. Your partner will understand how hard this is for you. Chances are, the subject has been avoided for a long, long time.

Your spouse's simple request may prove to be one of the most difficult assignments you have ever faced. But if it is important enough for your lover to mention, it is important enough for you to work on.

21

Unusual Requests

===//===

Now comes the part that makes life interesting. Each of us is different. Therefore, each of us has a different set of needs. One of the sure signs that sets extraordinary lovers apart from the garden variety of married couples is the delight they take in meeting each other's peculiar requests.

For instance: Some husbands like their wives to scratch their heads for them as they fall asleep...to wear white lipstick...to sing lullabies to them...to call their bosses for them when they have to miss work...to smile during lovemaking...to always meet them at the door with a long kiss and a warm embrace...to try a hair-color change ...to watch Sunday afternoon golf with them even though their wives have no interest in nor knowledge of the game... to wear nylons that require a garter belt rather than the much more practical panty hose...to join them for breakfast out-of-doors every summer morning, with the pollen, the humidity, and the bugs!

You think that's bad? Some wives like their husbands to tickle their backs until they get goose bumps...to buy them roses even though they have a dozen rose bushes in full bloom in the backyard ... to call them a dozen times a day ... to French kiss first thing in the morning even before they've had a chance to brush their teeth ... to always arrive ten minutes earlier than they promised to be there ... to wear pink pajamas ... to wear no pajamas ... to select the perfume they want them to wear ... to accompany them in the examining room for their doctors' appointments ... to say, "I love you," about 97 different times a day, even when other people are standing around!

Ordinary couples are scandalized by such requests. "No way!" they protest, shaking their heads vigorously. "That's ridiculous! That ... that's bizarre! You'll never get me to act like a fool for her! What if somebody found out?"

Thus most couples settle for mediocrity—worse, insist on it! No wonder such people are frequently tempted by the disastrous trap of extramarital affairs when they get bored while huddled in the tiny corner of their relationship they've painted themselves into. The only variety they've left themselves is a change of partner.

Ah, but the great lovers among us keep the home fires burning brightly not only by honoring our mates' unusual requests but by deliberately seeking them out! We are fascinated by the things about our spouses that make them special, that separate them from the crowd. We explore one another's whims, delights, and fantasies with the same excitement a spelunker greets a heretofore undiscovered room in a familiar cave.

If you should ever be so fortunate in your hour together as to hear from your spouse's lips a request that is decidedly unusual, a little whacky, even mind-bogglingly daring, thank God above for such an opportunity. So long as it involves just the two of you and hurts no one, go for it!

Your mate's fragile, secret person has sent out a single little probe to determine the hostility or safety of your marital atmosphere. If by enthusiastic reception you pass the test, that tiny probe will return to base with the message, "It's safe. You can come out now."

Perhaps for the first time in your marriage, you will get to meet the naked, defenseless, totally unique creation that has learned the hard way to stay hidden inside your spouse from the cold, harsh, judgmental world all these years. When that begins to happen, you can forget dull predictability, wide yawns, and stultifying boredom. Who knows? Your trembling, wounded psyche may work up the nerve to send out a tiny probe of its own one day.

Usually through no fault of their own, ordinary couples simply cannot loosen up. Past traumas or personality traits have paralyzed them with fear, in spite of the fact that very deep within them may be buried the genuine desire for marital openness. Unless they seek out competent, godly counsel to help them sort through their blockages, they may find themselves protesting the very lives they secretly wish they could lead. In such cases, they frequently behave as though an unseen jury hovers above them in the air at all times, ready to squelch any departures from the norm at a moment's notice.

"Where do you get these ideas of yours?" they demand, on those rare occasions when their mates make a shy request. "Do you lay awake at night by the hour thinking them up? Sheeesh! How many other men do that for their wives? For that matter, how many other wives would have the gall to ask that of their husbands? Sorry, Sweetheart, but I'm no weirdo. Forget it!"

What a triumphant closing argument. Ignoring decorum, the unseen "jury" stands, applauding wildly in unanimous agreement. The judge smashes down his gavel, declaring the defendant guilty!

And guilty she is—guilty of being honest about her desires... guilty of trusting her husband with her innermost secrets... guilty of hoping that her husband's love would make him want to do this special thing for her... guilty of attempting to nudge their relationship out of the same-as-the-day-before rut it is in.

But of one thing you can be sure, Mister Prosecuting Attorney: The defendant will never be found guilty of such a crime again.

"Would You Please Run That by Me One More Time?"

22

—#—

S o what do you do when your spouse takes no action on one of your requests?

First, be sure you have given your wife enough time to make the internal adjustments necessary. It is one thing for her to be able to conceptualize that a change needs to be made. It is quite another thing for her to be able to pull it off. Just because she hasn't acted on your request for two weeks doesn't necessarily mean she isn't going to. Be patient.

Suppose you take one of your turns during the hour to say, "I love surprises. Sometime I'd love for you to show up at my office unannounced and take me out to lunch... or to the museum for an art show... or home for a torrid love session!"

Not bad, not bad. That kind of behavior is the spice of lovers' lives. So the very next day you're on edge, wondering, "Is today the day?" Well, no it isn't. "Tomorrow then?" Not yet. "The day after?" Nothing.

"I can't believe she didn't take me seriously!" you may be tempted to moan. "In our next session I'd better tell her how important this is to me, or I'll never get surprised!"

Hold your horses. Give the woman a break. The very fact that you had to ask her to surprise you to begin with probably means she isn't exactly in the habit of arranging such events. In fact, it is just possible that she has never before in her life done what you have just asked her to do.

What's taking her so long? Well, for starters, she may be building up her courage. Or she may be struggling with the identity crisis your request has brought on, since she has never viewed herself as that type of person. For her to be effective in planning such an outing, you are going to need to give her time to work through her inner blockages until she is enthusiastic about it. The last thing you want is for her to go through the motions within 72 hours like an automaton, just because you are eager.

If in response to pressure from you she acts prematurely, her discomfort will show. It will lack the spontaneity and excitement you envisioned when you made your request, and your little lunchtime venture will probably be a flop. Neither of you will be eager to repeat the catastrophe, and the potential of your great idea will probably never be realized.

On the other hand, things might not be that serious. You asked to be surprised, so she may be waiting until you have given up expecting her to show up each day. Then as soon as she senses you've left for work not expecting to see each other until 6:00 P.M. that night, wham! She'll spring it on you!

So hang in there. Don't make the same request too often, even when no response seems forthcoming. That's nagging, and lovers seldom nag. It costs too much. Most lovers would rather have specific needs go unmet than introduce friction into their smoothly flowing relationships.

If a couple of months go by without a response, however, it's probably time to bring it up again. When a decent interval of time has passed, it's no longer nagging; instead, it's time to remind.

But when you do, be careful how you go about it. Be sure to save it for your one hour a week, even though to you it's "old" business. And when you bring it up, remember the rules: Do not get irritated and do not word it as a direct or implied complaint. You can say,

> Remember when I asked you to surprise me sometime during my lunch hour at the office? Sweetheart, that was two months ago! I've waited patiently. I've given you plenty of time to come up with an idea, and yet you've apparently ignored my request entirely! What's the problem, here? Do you just not want to do it, or what?

You can say that, but you're not going to like the result. In fact, if you want to be sure to kill your idea forever, that's exactly how to do it. A speech like that shouts your irritation, your suppressed anger. So before you raise the "surprise" issue a second time, be sure to get rid of all your negative emotions over it.

23

The
Mercy Game

*B*efore we go any further, let's take a break. Throughout this Secret you have been advised to get rid of your anger before you share your needs with your mate. That sounds hard, but it is even harder to actually do!

Allow me to suggest an enjoyable way to assist you in accomplishing that formidable task. It's called the "Mercy Game."

Here's how it's played. While eating lunch by yourself on one of those days you had hoped your wife would pop in and surprise you, walk it through:

> Okay. So she hasn't surprised me for lunch. Does that mean she doesn't love me? Doesn't respect me? Doesn't want to please me? Absurd. Of course she does. She's my lover.
>
> Then why hasn't she shown up? Well, maybe she couldn't come up with a good idea right away, and then she just forgot. Come to think of it, two months ago was her busiest time of year at work. She had to stay late three or four nights a week and take 20-

minute lunch breaks just to—oh, for crying out loud! That's it. For the first several weeks she had no opportunity to surprise me, and when the rush was over, she was mentally and physically exhausted. She hasn't purposely ignored me—she just forgot!

That's how you play the "Mercy Game." Actually, the "Mercy Game" is familiar to all of us—we are quick to play it in our own behalf where our own behavior is concerned! By implementing its familiar principles in your spouse's behalf, it enables you to get rid of any residual bitterness you may be harboring before you make your second request. Keep walking it through until you arrive at a plausible, "merciful" explanation for your spouse's behavior.

It doesn't matter whether or not your solution is precisely correct in all details. Who besides God can read someone else's mind? The important thing for you to see is that there is at least one legitimate explanation for your wife's inaction on your request. And if you can come up with one, you can probably come up with a dozen, if you care to take the time.

So since you have the option of assigning to your darling either a charitable motive or an uncharitable motive, which one do you think a genuine lover is going to select? Right. Now all that remains is for you to decide whether or not you are a genuine lover.

24

If at First You Don't Succeed...

W hen you are finally ready, take a different approach than the one you took the first time. In spite of the fact that it has been two months since you asked your wife to surprise you for lunch, don't repeat yourself. If you use the same words it will still come across as nagging—or even worse, as an insult.

Besides, for whatever reason, your first stab at it didn't work, remember? Spend the extra planning time it takes to come up with a new angle. After all, if it is important enough for you to bring up again, it is important enough for you to handle better the second time.

You might approach it like this:

> Remember when I asked you to surprise me at lunch a couple of months ago? Well, I've got an even better idea. I got to thinking it was unfair of me to ask you to do something I hadn't done myself. So why don't I show you what I have in mind by surprising you first?
>
> One of these days during the next two weeks I'll just show up at your office, sweep

you off your feet, and take you to Never-Never Land for the next hour! We'll have a fabulous time, I promise. Then, once we've both thoroughly enjoyed ourselves and you can begin to see the possibilities, you'll have two weeks to show up and surprise me.

We'll take turns! This way we'll both have a couple of daytime pick-me-ups to look forward to each month, but it won't work a hardship on either one of us. What do you say?

In most cases, that will do the trick. Your wife will be perfectly aware that you had to ask her twice, but she will note that you did so without complaint or anger. She will also note that you spent some time looking at it from her point of view. Finally, the mere idea that you brought it up twice with such consideration and care shows her how important it is to you, and how much you value that time with her. Better hang on to your hat, Bub. You're probably in for a surprising lunch a few weeks from now!

"But what if I'm not?" you may ask. "What if I do my part and surprise her, but she doesn't go along with my request and surprise me?"

That's a very real possibility. If she failed to follow through the first time, there is a stronger-than-average chance that the same thing will happen again. For some reason known only to her and God, the blockage inside her may be that great.

In that case, here is what you as a lover should do. During the very next one-hour session after her two weeks are up, it is time to bring up the subject again. The past three months have been a test of her ability to become someone that she simply may not now have the capacity to be. But today is a test of your love for her.

Once again, before you approach her on this, be sure you have rid yourself of all negative emotions, including blame, resentment, and disappointment. Then tell her,

> Darling, I want to begin today by withdrawing one of my requests. When I asked you to surprise me at lunch, I was thinking more of myself than of you. I should have known better. That's just not your style. And do you know what? I like you just exactly the way you are. So as of this moment forward, that request no longer exists.
>
> Since we had such a great time when I surprised you for lunch a couple of weeks ago, I think I'd like to keep doing that now and then, if you don't mind. I can't tell you how much I really enjoy doing things like that, and I can tell you like it, too.

Please don't say this to her unless you can say it from your heart. But since you are a lover rather than a fighter, if you really work at it, you'll find that it is well within your capacity to do so.

Why should you give in on something this important to you? Because as a lover, your highest priority, your strongest motivation, your greatest thrill is not getting your own way. It is pleasing your mate.

Besides, this approach isn't quite as sacrificial as it sounds. In fact, it happens to be the wisest thing you could ever do. In effect, you have learned that when it comes to surprising you for lunch, she doesn't respond to pressure. But for all you know, once the pressure is removed she may be freed up to do the very thing you asked!

There are no guarantees, of course. But think it through. She does love you with all her heart—that you are sure of. And even though she finds it extremely hard to do, still she knows that if she can ever work up enough courage to try it, she will blow your mind. Talk about surprising you for lunch!

So as is always the case, the right approach is also the smartest approach. If you ever have a prayer of getting that surprise lunch, this is the way to go about it.

But don't hold your breath. Just continue to surprise her, making sure the times you share together are a beautiful experience. You promised her that your request was no longer in effect, so be sure you keep your promise. Put it out of your mind.

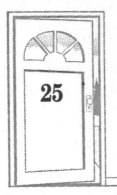

What About Requests You Cannot Morally Honor?

25

Although you are lovers, there is always the chance—slim though it may be—that one of you will accidentally take a detour at some point in your marriage and leave the main path. Unthinkable as it may now seem to you, crises similar to the one I am about to describe have befallen seemingly "perfect" marriages. Although you may never have to face something this catastrophic in your own relationship, perhaps you can glean from it helpful principles that may one day help guide you through a less-traumatic but nevertheless difficult situation.

Let us suppose that you and your husband gratefully enjoy a healthy, creative sexual relationship. As with many of God's blessings, however, there is a fine line between freedom and license. For purposes of illustration, we'll let the man take the role of the spouse who, in his exuberance, temporarily crosses that sexual line. The wife will assume the role of the offended party.

It all started so innocently. Following an especially playful lovemaking session, you were relaxing in each others' arms, engaging in your usual loving banter.

"Wow!" your husband exclaimed. "You were great tonight, do you know that?"

"You weren't so bad yourself," you replied. "...for a beginner."

"For a 'beginner'!" your husband scoffed. "Listen to you! So what do you call yourself: an expert?"

"That's right," you answered. "I have an earned doctorate in Advanced Lovemaking."

"So where did you do all your 'research'?"

"Wouldn't you like to know?" you shot back. And then, "Oops, I didn't mean that. Sorry. You do know where I did my research: with you—and only you."

"No way!" your husband protested. "I'm not letting you off that easily! Come clean now. With whom else did you do all that research?"

"With no one else! You know that. Stop it now."

"Okay, okay," your husband said. Then his voice took on a different tone. "But you can't tell me you haven't thought about it."

"Thought about what?" you asked, vaguely bothered by the turn your conversation had taken.

"You know, thought about what it would be like...with someone else."

"I don't appreciate your insinuation," you replied, pulling away from him slightly.

"Oh, come on, Honey," he said. "Everybody thinks about it from time to time."

"Including you?"

"Sure, I'll admit it. What's the big deal? There's no harm in just thinking."

"I can't believe what I'm hearing," you said, pulling yourself up in bed to face him. "I can't believe I just heard my husband tell me that he imagines 'what it would be like' with another woman!"

"Well, haven't you?"

"No!" you exploded.

"I don't believe you," your husband said flatly. "You're just afraid to admit it, that's all. You're making me out to be the bad guy, when you've done the same thing. You're being a hypocrite about this, and that's unfair to me."

Somewhat taken aback, you replied, "What I meant is, I refuse to entertain those kinds of thoughts."

"But you have had them."

"Not really," you protested.

"What's this 'Not really' business?" your husband asked and shook his head sarcastically. "You've either thought about what it would be like with another man or you haven't. Which is it?"

"What has got into you?" you demanded.

"I just don't think it's healthy to hide it from each other, that's all. It's a perfectly normal thing to look at someone who interests you and wonder what they'd be like in bed. That's all I'm saying. I'm sorry that you are unwilling to be honest with me about your own thoughts."

"Forget my thoughts," you snapped. "So who have you thought about?"

"I'll tell you, if you tell me."

"I have nothing to tell!"

"You mean you have nothing you *will* tell," your husband replied quietly.

"You're scaring me, you know that?" you told him. "Thinking about going to bed with someone else is the first step toward doing it."

"So?"

"What do you mean, 'So?'" you replied, flabbergasted. "Are you telling me that you have considered actually going to bed with someone else?"

"I would never do anything behind your back," your husband answered.

"Oh, but you would do it in front of my face?"

"Don't be absurd. I meant I would never do anything without your consent."

"'Without my consent'," you echoed hollowly.

"Are you saying you would *with* my consent?"

Your husband muttered something under his breath in reply.

"What did you say?"

"Nothing."

"Yes, you did. You said something. What did you say?"

Long pause. Then, "I said, 'Only if it was mutual.'"

You are sick to your stomach. An eerie feeling of unreality has settled like a fog over your brain. This cannot be happening to you. "Please God, let it be a dream! Let it be a horrible nightmare, and let me wake up this very minute!"

But it isn't, and you don't. Your husband is lying there in your marriage bed with a guilty look on his face. Less than ten minutes before, you gave yourself to this man with abandon: heart, body, and soul. And now you have just heard him admit that he is open to sharing you with some other man just so he can have some other woman.

You feel devalued beyond words. He has just taken everything in your relationship that you hold dear, smeared it with sewage, and hurled it back in your face.

Worried that he has gone too far, your husband tries to soothe you. "Honey? Just forget it, okay? Just forget what I said. I didn't mean anything by it. Really."

Your eyes meet, and that is when from somewhere inside you the rage begins to build with something near the ferocity of a wounded she-bear. And you thought the two of you were lovers! Every ounce of affection you felt for him earlier has turned into utter loathing. You could scratch his filthy eyes out.

Buy Some Time

*I*f your spouse should ever ask you to do something you know to be biblically wrong, you may be tempted to lash out in anger. But don't. Wait until you have regained enough of your composure to speak in the most normal voice you can muster, and buy some time. "I need a little while to think. Could we please come back to this tomorrow?"

He may badger you for an answer and want a clue as to your initial reaction. But don't give it to him. Tell him you need to be left alone until tomorrow so you can think. Period.

If you need to cry, get in the car, drive to somewhere safe and private, and release the flood that has built up inside you. Something very precious to you has just died. You are in mourning. You have every right to weep over your incalculable loss.

But then it is time to get hold of yourself. This is no time for you to go limp with self-pity. Most definitely it is not the time to go running to your best friend, your parents, or his. If necessary, there will be plenty of time for that later. But for now, this is nobody else's business but yours and your husband's. If the damage can be repaired just between the two of you, then that is where it needs to stop.[1]

Your first step is to pray as you have never prayed before. Ask God to awaken your husband from the trance into which he has fallen. Ask God also for wisdom, for strength ... and for the right words, at the right time. If you know of someone else who can really pray, ask them to get busy, but do not give them any details whatsoever. God will know, and that is all that matters for now. Just tell them it very personal and very important. If they become too nosy, you have selected the wrong person.

It is essential that you now assume command of the situation. For whatever reason, your husband has been temporarily incapacitated, as surely as though he had suffered a stroke. You dare not allow it to continue, for this is far more than an everyday sexual request. Your marriage is at stake. Fight for it.

You must then get rid of the rage that threatens to consume you. Yes, what your husband has suggested is detestable. Yes, you may feel he deserves to be force-fed a live grenade. But you would end up being the one who had to clean up the mess! This is no time for destruction. Enough of that has already occurred.

Instead, now is the time for you to do the best clear-headed thinking you have ever done in your life, and you need an anger-free mind to do it with. So pull out the Mercy Game and start playing. Only this time it is no game. It is deadly serious. You must play the Mercy Game to win. For example, if your husband's request falls into the category of sexual sin, as mentioned in Doorway 25, ask yourself:

> Why would he do this to me? We have a fan-
> tastic sex life! It's not as if he has been deprived

in that area! Okay, that's part of it. We're always looking for ways to make our sex life better, and my dear, dumb-dumb husband has just crossed the line that divides insatiability from insanity. He probably actually thinks this will push us to a new level of sexual excitement.

If I ever doubted the existence of Satan, I doubt it no longer. I feel his malevolent attack against the sacredness of our marriage as certainly as I have ever felt anything in my life!

And I doubt that Satan did it without help. Who was it who fed this kind of trash into my husband's mind? Where in the world would he pick up this kind of twisted thinking? Was it somebody at work? Somebody at the club? A book or a magazine? Has he got a stash of pornography somewhere?

Did he see something on television, could it be— oh no! That movie I picked up at the video store and wanted him to watch with me last month! Ellen recommended it as a great love story, but it did have that one part in it between the man and this woman he met at a party while his wife was out of town. Come to think of it, the movie portrayed that one-night stand as the steamiest encounter of the whole story. Great. Looks like I helped slit my own throat.

Are there any positives in this mess? Well, for one, apparently he hasn't done anything with anyone. There's that much. For another, he discussed it with me. That means he isn't trying to hide anything. For that matter, it means he's trying to do it within the context of our marriage, rather than outside it.

So what have I got, here? I've got a foolish
husband whose train has jumped the track, that's
what I've got. He's probably been bombarded lately
with an unusual amount of dangerous input—some
of which I was personally responsible for bringing
into our home!

This is the biggest challenge of our marriage,
true. But this is not the end of the world. We can
beat this—and we're going to!

Continue to wrestle with the problem until you have it
pinned to the mat. You will know you have succeeded when
you have totally forgiven your husband for his foolishness
and when you have a clear plan of action for tomorrow.

When the hour arrives the next day, take charge from
the start. Do not raise your voice, but do not allow him to
interrupt you. Look him straight in the eye, and if he drops
his gaze, ask him to look at you so you can speak from your
heart.

I regard the wife-swapping suggestion you made
yesterday as the worst mistake you have ever
made in your life. The answer to your hinting
around is "No." I will never have sex with another
man nor give you permission to have sex with
another woman as long—I repeat—as long as we
are married. Your contemplation of it has
dishonored me and has desecrated the sanctity of
our relationship.

I know you didn't come up with this on your
own. Your love for me is too strong, too pure. If the
movie I brought home last month contributed to
your current mind-set, I accept that portion of the
blame. But the rest of it is between you and God. I

don't know who you've been listening to, but I want you to end that relationship *now*. I don't know what literature you've been reading, what tapes you've been hearing, or what videos you've been watching, but I want you to get rid of them immediately. That is not a request. That is a demand.

Sweetheart, I beg you to do as Colossians Chapter 3 says: Take off your old self with all its evil, and put on your new Christian self, which is who you really are![2] Honey, I'm susceptible to the same temptations. That's what I have to do—that's what *we* have to do!

Now, let me make myself perfectly clear, just so you know where we stand. If you even so much as hint at anything like this ever again, I will go straight for help to the most godly couple I can think of in our church, and I will ask them to meet with us until we have this problem resolved. If you refuse to listen to them, I will be forced to take this issue to our pastor for advice. So please consider this to be your last and only warning.

Finally, I do not want to hear one word from you on this subject unless it begins with a heartfelt, down-to-the-bone apology. I took 24 hours to think over my reply to you, and I want you to take 24 hours to think over your reply to me. Frankly, I do not want to hear one word from you right now. It would come too cheaply, and the cost you have already forced me to pay is too dear.

On the other hand, you may not want to beat around the bush like that. You may want to just tell him what you think!

"But what happened to the concept of sharing needs instead of complaints?" you may ask.

Legitimate question. My reply is that moral issues such as wife-swapping, adultery, fraud, tax evasion, theft, lying, and murder must be handled with the shock value of a strong rebuke. This is how Paul treated the apostle Peter, when Peter briefly slipped into a hypocritical life-style at Antioch.[3] Ideally, such issues should be dealt with so decisively and effectively that they are unlikely ever to be brought up again.

There is no place in lovers' lives for moral compromise. Wholly apart from issues of right and wrong, it will undermine the integrity of your entire relationship. Waste no time discussing whether or not you will be honest this week or whether you should go shoplifting together. There are some things that simply are not debatable.

Instead, spend time together in Bible study as a couple. And make sure you focus on those portions of Scripture that spell out the holy life-style to which God calls us as His children. Your husband may bring up to you the scriptural admonition that wives should submit to their husbands.[4] Certainly, you should acknowledge your whole-hearted acceptance of that principle. But then you must explain to him that issues of right and wrong are no longer solely between the two of you as husband and wife, but also between each of you and God—and your obedience to God takes precedence over your obedience to your husband!

One example of this is Jesus' clear command to His disciples: "The teachers of the law and the Pharisees sit in Moses' seat. So you must obey them and do everything they tell you."[5]

But when the apostles were brought before the entire Sanhedrin, the high priest gave them a command that conflicted with the higher command of God: "We gave you strict orders not to teach in this name."

Notice the apostles' response: "We must obey God rather than men!"[6]

If you and your husband continue to disagree over the scriptural interpretation and application of these kinds of passages, call on a godly person or couple who are mature, full of wisdom, and rock-solid in their commitment to God's Word. Ask them to join you some evening for Bible study, and invite their input.

Should you actually come on as strongly as we suggest? Ultimately, nobody can answer that for you, because no one but you will be forced to live with the consequences. You must be yourself, as the Holy Spirit directs you. But of this you can be sure: You dare not treat lightly such a threat to all you—and your God—hold dear.

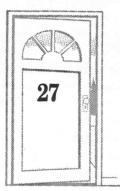

What About Requests to Which You Are Strongly Opposed?

27

As we have just seen, some issues are cut-and-dried. Other issues, however, fall into the category of "cut-but-still-damp."

Only rarely in a lovers' relationship will you be forced to confront a dilemma so clearly one-sided as wife-swapping. Far more common will be ambiguous issues about which you both feel strongly—but in opposite directions. These can feel to each of you like moral principles, but really they are not. They are strongly held convictions, and it is vital that you be able to tell the difference.

For example, out of the clear blue your wife may announce, "Darling, we need to find a good sitter for our baby so I can go back to school and get my degree in Marketing."

Your wife may be convinced that she has a responsibility to fully develop her academic potential. You, however, may have strong feelings that her rightful place is in the home until your child is old enough to go to school.

Does her request fall into the category of a moral imperative? That is, would it be wrong under all circumstances for her to put off the resumption of her degree work for another five years? No, morally it would not.

"That's it!" you may conclude triumphantly. "There's our answer! She's only thinking of the short-term sense of accomplishment she would feel to get college behind her. I'm thinking of the long-term impact on our child!"

Not so fast, Mr. Traditionalist. What if (God forbid!) you should become disabled while your child is still at home? Such things do happen to big, strong men like you. Suddenly, your wife's degree wouldn't look so frivolous to you, would it? It could make the difference between keeping or losing your home . . . between being able to afford or having to pass up the specialized health care you need. Now whose thinking appears short-term and whose is taking the long-term view?

Let's take a look at another burning issue of our times. Suppose your husband tenderly wraps his arms around you and softly whispers in your ear, "Sweetheart, I need to spend $7,800 of our savings on a big-screen TV."

He is thinking of all those baseball, basketball, and football games and of their, ah, educational benefit for the whole family. You, on the other hand, may firmly believe that your savings should never be dipped into, except in a dire emergency.

"No contest!" you may protest. "His position is totally indefensible. All he wants to do is sit in his recliner for the entire weekend, watching his ball games while the yard-work goes undone, the house falls down around our ears, and the rest of us in the family have to fend for ourselves, totally ignored. His request is utterly selfish."

And you could be right. But probably you are not. He's your lover, remember? This is not Beer-Belly Bobby who lives down the street that we're discussing. This is the man who sweetly bathed your brow every morning when you were deathly sick during your first pregnancy. This is the man who has carefully studied your responses so thoroughly that he can transport you to another planet with his lovemaking. This is the man who, if called upon, would literally lay down his life for you. And all he wants is a TV.

Sure, it's a stupid expenditure. But lovers have been known to be foolishly extravagant in the way they occasionally lavish large gifts upon one another. That kind of openheartedness is usually returned, with interest. Lovers love the giver more than the gift. You just may end up with more grass mowed, more leaky faucets fixed, and more attention paid to you and the kids by this man whom you've made to feel so deeply valued, so wildly loved.

Will it knock a huge hole in your carefully laid retirement budget? Yup. But what if your precious hubby drops dead of a heart attack one year before you go on that cruise around the world? Such things do happen to big, strong men like him, you know. As you stand there peering down into the casket, you wouldn't be the first widow who suddenly had it pop into her mind, "I wish I had let you have that dumb TV."

Here's the guideline: If by considering the matter through the eyes of your mate you can see there actually exists another legitimate side, then loosen up. Life's short. Pleasing your mate every chance you get is no crime. That's what lovers do.

If your wife really wants to go back to school this fall, you ought to move heaven and earth to see that she has that opportunity. She's no ogre. She's a wonderful mother. She's not about to deprive her baby of the love and care her little bundle of joy needs. Together you can come up with a plan that you, your wife, and your child can thrive on.

Does your husband think he really has to have that monstrous screen wedged into your tiny den? Then why not brainstorm with him how you can knock out a wall somewhere and adjust your budget so you can afford to purchase the TV within a reasonable time—but without putting the family under undue stress or failing to take into consideration what you would do if something happened to him. Be sure, too, that somewhere in your discussion your husband gets to ponder the reality that while "things" can enhance the happiness that already exists, "things" cannot buy happiness that isn't already there.

In the course of running the numbers and weighing all priorities, your husband may shake his head and conclude, "This is stupid. We can't do this now."

But if he doesn't, and if one day you do stand peering down into his casket, don't be surprised if suddenly through the tears you smile and say, "You precious man. I'm so glad I let you get that dumb TV."

Some Helpful Pointers

*T*he following suggestions will help you get the most out of your weekly hour together.

1. *Don't interrupt your mate.* You have only one hour, so remain quiet and listen while your spouse is speaking. You cannot afford to waste time by replying prematurely or by butting in with questions before your spouse has finished.

For some people this rule is nothing but common courtesy, easily observed. But for others, it appears to be well-nigh impossible. In that case, buy a book, listen to a tape, or enroll in a course that will train you how to be a good listener. Then put what you have learned into practice.

2. *Take notes.* This is important. It tells your wife that you value what she says. When your lover sees you scribbling furiously away while she shares her needs, it gives her confidence that you are actually going to do something about them.

But that's not all. You need those notes! They will provide you a checklist to work from each morning to be sure you meet all her requests. You dare not allow one of her needs to go unmet simply because it slipped your mind. You may forget...but she won't.

Take notes even if your memory is normally flawless. After all, even though you are lovers, these are the areas you've obviously been missing it on. Otherwise, she wouldn't have had to bring them up! Therefore, the issues she has had to raise represent your blind spots. Writing them down highlights them so you will be reminded to give them the extra attention they deserve.

Lastly, the process of taking notes will give you something positive to do while your mate speaks. Having an activity for your hands will make it easier to resist the temptation to interrupt. There is something about the process of moving pen across paper that helps keep you objective and nonreactionary while your mate is speaking. And there will be days when you will need all the help you can get!

3. *Don't cheat.* Except in true emergencies, do not bring up your relationship problems with your husband at other times. This will defeat the purpose of your special hour together, and you both will soon revert to the daily "Hack! Chop!" of ordinary relationships.

True emergencies are rare. Some examples? When you're seriously contemplating suicide...when you're on a crying jag and can't stop no matter how hard you try... when you feel like filing for divorce and find yourself flipping through the Yellow Pages in search of a really vicious attorney. Those are emergencies.

4. *Make it a high priority.* I don't care how busy you are, schedule around it. Any 60-minute period that buys you marital peace for the other 167 hours a week deserves to be guarded with your life!

When one of you has to be out of town, keep your appointment by phone. Don't let anything intrude during this sacred time except by mutual agreement when you have no choice. Even then, don't skip a week. Immediately reschedule it to fall as close to the original time as possible.

5. *Save it for your relationship.* This hour cannot be used to bring up problems of all kinds. There just isn't time. If you need to discuss Andy's grades in math, redecorating the living room, how you are going to rid your lawn of crabgrass, or even whether or not to file bankruptcy, do it on another occasion. Your relationship must remain your top priority. When things are right between the two of you, everything else falls into place.

6. *Relax.* Once you have shared your need, it's out of your hands. For now you have done everything you can do. You have watched him write down your request. So from this moment forward the matter has been passed to the care of your husband, who is the only person who can do anything about it, anyway. Release it! You'll be more content, and he'll do a better job without sensing that you are breathing down his neck.

What can you do during this time? You can pray for your husband as the spiritual leader of your family. You can ask God to communicate to him what you do not have the ability to convey. And finally, having done so, you can relax still further, knowing that you have entrusted your need to the highest power of all.

7. *Prioritize.* So what if you don't get to everything in one hour this week? Sixty minutes' worth of assignments is all most people can work on effectively anyway! No one can deal with everything at once—it becomes emotionally overwhelming. Save the rest until next week. So long as

you are certain that you have addressed the most important issues first, you can know that you are staying right on schedule.

Prioritizing forces you to tackle the underlying issues, rather than an unending stream of isolated incidents. As a result, you will eventually catch up and end up much farther along than when you were spatting every time you experienced an irritation.

Believe it or not, the day may come when you use your turn to reveal, "I can honestly say that the only thing I need from you this week is for you to keep right on doing what you're doing. I'm a very happy, contented woman!"

Then what will you do with the remaining time? I'm sure you'll think of something!

8. *Apologize from your heart.* When the hour is up, it's time to ask one another's forgiveness. Go over your notes (Already you are glad you took them!) and identify every single area that even remotely calls for an apology:

> Sweetheart, I'm sorry for not realizing how much you need me to touch you even when we're not leading up to lovemaking. Will you forgive me for having such a one-track mind and being so insensitive to your needs?

Especially apologize for what your spouse has had to bring up for the second or third time:

> Darling, I am so sorry for being late again this week and not calling. I want to be on time for you, above all people. I'm not going to offer you any excuse. I'm just going to work twice as hard on it from now on. Will you please forgive me for letting you down again?

Whatever you do, don't tack on an excuse. Let your spouse know what is going on in your life, certainly, but don't tell your wife, "Honey, I'm sorry for being grouchy when I get home from work, but the stress I'm under right now is unbelievable!"

That kind of halfhearted effort is totally unacceptable. She won't feel like she has heard you say you're sorry at all. You started out with an apology, certainly, but in the same breath you took it right back! It sounds like you are saying that you have every right to be a bear when you walk in that door.

And don't end up placing partial blame on your spouse, either. Don't tell her, "I'm sorry for my bad attitude when I get home, but sometimes you're in a bad mood yourself! It's pretty hard to get along with someone who is already on edge!"

Take full responsibility for your own actions. Let your apology stand alone, naked, without excuse. It's tougher that way, but it is far more satisfying to your spouse. And you'll feel better about yourself afterward.

Finally, allow your apology to come from your heart, not merely from your lips. Although you will be referring to your notes, don't keep your head buried in them when you speak. Your spouse won't get nearly as much from it if you do.

Take a deep breath and look your spouse in the eye when you apologize, even though it may be uncomfortable for you. It had better be! If you could glibly sail right through a string of "I'm sorries," your spouse would have good reason to question your sincerity. A heartfelt apology is always difficult...but always worth the effort.

9. *Forgive from your heart.* This is not the occasion for skeptical looks or for sarcastic phrases such as, "Well, it's about time!"

Be generous. Let your body language, your words, and your facial expressions make it clear to your spouse that you accept the apology and that all is forgiven.

You may say, "Thank you, Sweetheart, I do forgive you." As long as you look your spouse in the eye and communicate genuine sincerity, sometimes a simple "Okay" or even a meaningful nod works just as well.

One caution: Lovers sometimes make the mistake of saying things like, "Never mind, it was no big deal." That sounds generous, certainly. But one of the problems with that approach is that it devalues your husband's apology. He has gone through that entire healthy process of feeling genuinely remorseful, getting up his courage, and taking full responsibility for his own behavior. Then you come back with a contrary message that, in effect, tells him all his effort was a waste of time!

The truth is, there is no excuse for rude, inconsiderate, insensitive behavior, so don't make an excuse up. After your spouse has had the guts to say "I'm sorry," give him or her full credit for what has just been done. It *is* a big deal. Allow it to remain that way.

10. *End with a kiss and a warm embrace.* For lovers, this one is self-explanatory. I have every confidence that you can take it from here!

29

Lest You Misunderstand

=====//=====

All by itself, the Secret we have just shared with you can lift your marriage into the realm of greatness.

There is one thing that is vital for you to remember, however. This Secret works only when it is adopted by mutual consent. Neither of you can afford to be halfhearted or lackadaisical about implementing its principles. Otherwise, it is a prescription for marital disaster. That is why this book is titled *For Lovers Only*.

Even if you are delighted with this concept, be absolutely certain that your spouse shares your delight—and is faithfully implementing the principles contained herein. Properly used, this Secret is an amazingly effective strategy for dealing with your marital problems. Improperly used, however, it can become a vehicle for avoiding your problems and allowing bitterness to accumulate day after day.

If you find yourself remaining upset with your spouse while you wait for your one-hour meeting to arrive, go back to the beginning of this Secret and reenter the Doorways that show you how to get rid of your hurt or your anger. You may find, however, that your habit patterns have been etched too deeply to allow you to change. In that case, you are better off to admit it to your spouse and together work out a compromise plan that both of you can live with.

The same holds true when you can tell that your spouse is having difficulty between meetings. If you suspect that your spouse has a problem of any size with you—small, medium, or large—go to her immediately. Do not wait for your meeting, as you would normally do when you are the one who has the problem. Drop whatever else you are doing and immediately take the steps necessary to effect reconciliation.[1]

You might say, "Sweetheart, is anything bothering you?"

If she denies it, be sure that she isn't covering up out of embarrassment that she cannot get rid of her hurt or her anger without your help.

You might volunteer, "Why don't we call an emergency session and discuss it? Something tells me this isn't going to go away unless we give it special attention."

Your sensitivity to her upset and your willingness to call a special session may make the difference for her. She may respond, "No, I think I'm going to be all right, Darling. Thank you for offering. It will be much better if we save it for our regular session. I've got some more homework to do before I'm ready to discuss it."

In that case, so long as you are convinced she really means it, honor her request. If you barge ahead anyway, you may end up regretting it.

On the other hand, she may gratefully acknowledge her need to talk it out before your next scheduled session. By all means, do. If it is possible, she should observe the principle of sharing her need, rather than lodging her complaint. If she is too distraught to do so, however, make the best of it, even if everything collapses and you end up fumbling through it in the old-fashioned way.

You are human beings, after all, not robots. From time to time old habit patterns will suddenly pop up and refuse to go away—especially when you are tired or are experiencing an unusual amount of stress. During such periods, you may end up having two or three sessions a week. If so, don't worry about it. That still beats arguing all the time.

Besides, you don't have to do what anybody else says, and that includes the authors of this book. With God's help, the two of you are still the only true "experts" when it comes to your marriage.

30 This Isn't So Radical After All, Is It?

=====#=====

B efore you explored this Secret, doing all your quarreling in one hour a week sounded awfully radical, didn't it? But the farther you read, the more familiar it began to sound...as familiar, in fact, as the Bible.

Let us leave you with these verses of Scripture, and see if they don't beautifully sum up the spirit of what you have just read.

> But the fruit of the Spirit is love, joy, peace, patience, kindness, goodness, faithfulness, gentleness and self-control. Against such things there is no law. Those who belong to Christ Jesus have crucified the sinful nature with its passions and desires. Since we live by the Spirit, let us keep in step with the Spirit. Let us not become conceited, provoking and envying each other.[1]

> Love is patient, love is kind. It does not envy, it does not boast, it is not proud. It is not rude, it is not self-seeking, it is not easily angered, it keeps no record of wrongs. Love

does not delight in evil but rejoices with the truth. It always protects, always trusts, always hopes, always perseveres. Love never fails.[2]

Secret
Number Two

Make Love
in the
Garden of Eden!

Incontrovertible Proof: There Is a God!

Anybody who has ever experienced great lovemaking instinctively knows the truth: Sex is too good to have just happened. It didn't evolve as the result of some cosmic accident. Something this exquisite had to have been lovingly, brilliantly, creatively designed.

If an atheist ever comes up to you and demands proof that there is a God, all you have to answer is one word: "Sex." Give him a day to think about it. If at the end of that day he remains unconvinced, then he has just revealed far more about his sex life—or the lack thereof—than he ever intended!

God created sex. Doesn't that tell you a lot about who God really is? Among other things, it tells you that He is ingenious.

Imagine Adam's and Eve's bodies without any sexual characteristics. God says to Himself, "All right. There they are, created in My image...but not quite. I want to give them the ability to express their love to one another in a way that will arouse all the wonder and excitement of this moment of creation for the rest of their lives.

"I've got it! I'll design their bodies so that they can literally become one. I'll give them a tangible way to bridge the gap of loneliness they will feel, and to enable them, whenever they choose, to lose themselves in one another.

"After they fall, their lives are going to be full of challenges, of heartaches, of pain, of intense stress. So I'll build into their times of oneness the potential for healing, for release, for total intimacy, and for an excitement that utterly surpasses the intensity of the stress they have been called upon to bear.

"And then, to flood them with awe, I will grant them at the precise moment of their greatest transport the capacity to create another human being!"

What a concept! What a mind-blowing invention! But at the same time, what a challenge. Think of all the engineering problems He had to solve in order to bring it off!

And did He ever solve them! God pulled out all the stops when He invented sex. Here He shows off His artistry like nowhere else. The instruments of love He designed are a never-ceasing source of wonder. They are so soft, and yet so strong. They are so tender, so sensitive to the touch, so utterly vulnerable. And yet, only moments later they can withstand an amazing physical assault that culminates not in pain but in wave after wave of indescribable pleasure!

Its basics are so simple that if you could find a newly-wed couple who had never heard a single word of instruction, they would still be able to figure it out for themselves. The more their love grew, the more it would cry out to be expressed physically, until, in the agony and intensity of their desire for one another, they would discover the way to become one, as though they alone had just invented sex.

And yet, the infinite complexity of our sexuality continues to baffle even those who have devoted a lifetime of study to its mysteries. There are no sex experts. There are only children, playing with God's most fascinating creation.

Go with us, then, as we enter this very secret, very private, very intimate realm where lovers come alive. But let us enter gently, reverently, in the soft, hushed tones of those who realize we are in the presence of greatness.

In the following pages you will find absent the animalism of pornographic crudity. But absent also will be the blindness of stifling prudery.

Instead we will proceed with clarity, with openness, and with a sense of excitement as we explore the hidden potential God has secreted in the heart of your marriage.

Ours will be a return to the Garden of Eden... without the shame, without the blame... with only the wonder.

The man and his wife were both naked,
and they felt no shame.

—Genesis 2:25

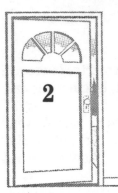

2 Please Read This First: A Word of Caution

==== # ====

*L*et me begin by reminding you that this book is different. It is intended for married couples who are already lovers, but who want to see how greatly they can intensify their love.

They are the kind of people who are mildly offended by the word "mild." They are the sort who experiment with different spices in their favorite foods and who love to try new, exotic dishes—even if they end up leaving half the food uneaten on their plates!

It's not that they aren't content—just the opposite. They are so pleased with what they have that they assume there must be more where this came from!

They are the curious, the playful, the experimenters, the adventurers among us. When they pass by a cave, they want to see what's inside. When some new car owner shows them the big engine under his hood, they wonder how fast it will go. When a member of the group points out a little path that winds off into the woods, they are tempted to leave the tour and find out where it leads.

They are not reckless. Instead, they are reasonable risk-takers. They know they will occasionally get burned, but to them, within certain limits, it is worth it. In wisdom, they have already eliminated the possibility of second- and third-degree burns before going in. But to enable them to keep stretching, growing, feeling, experiencing, they are willing to suffer a few blisters from time to time.

Have I just described you? If not, Judy and I would like to request that you not read this section. You are likely to be deeply offended, and we wish to avoid that at all costs. We want to be a help, not a hindrance. We want to provide you with stepping-stones, not to impede your path with stumbling blocks.

This book is for lovers only. In particular, this section of the book is for couples who already have a good sex life and who want to see how much better it can get. For us to be a help to you, we are going to have to take some risks. Our greatest risks are with four kinds of people.

The first is the person who has picked up this book with a negative agenda. This kind of person will ignore all of our cautions and warnings—including this one. He will read *For Lovers Only* not to be helped, but to hurt. Out of the agony of his own damaged personality, this person will twist our words, run roughshod over our loving intent, and attack us viciously for our sexual openness.

The second major risk we run is with the person who does not share our understanding of God's marvelous gift of sex. This person may think sex is basically dirty; therefore, she concludes that anyone who writes about sex is dirty, too.

Thirdly, there is the kind of person who may think that sex is wonderful but so private that one should never seek advice or counsel in order to make it even more wonderful.

Finally, there is the person whose list of acceptable sex practices is very short. It is inevitable, therefore, that he will be scandalized by a book specifically designed to show couples that their list of pure, wholesome sexual options is instead virtually unlimited.

A number of years ago, Judy and I took a group of about 40 husbands and wives on a "For Lovers Only" advance. (We don't like to go on "retreats"—the kind of conference we prefer to conduct is an "advance.") As we do in this book, we warned the participants before they signed up that we were going to be open and frank.

Just before we began the sexual loving portion of our seminar, we took a 15-minute break and asked everyone who had even the remotest possibility of being offended to please skip the next segment. We suggested they use the time to relax in their rooms, to read, to meditate, to talk, or to take a walk in the woods instead. Everyone returned for the next session. But one of the couples shouldn't have.

To this day, we do not know if this couple attended the seminar from the very start with a negative agenda, or if they simply did not know how to follow instructions. But this we do know: Upon their return to the city, they criticized us everywhere they went for the explicit nature of our sexual instruction.

The Scripture says,

> Do not throw your pearls to pigs. If you do,
> they may trample them under their feet. . . . [1]

Judy and I regard what we are about to share with you as very special and precious. To us, each of the Doorways in this Secret is a "pearl" of liberating, godly counsel.

As you will discover in the pages that follow, we despise sexual sin. But we are also convinced that a boring, unimaginative sex life leads to marital dissatisfaction and eventually to unfulfillment, even in the best of relationships. It is then that the deceptive "excitement" of an extramarital affair can begin to look more and more attractive.

The best way to prevent your mate from being tempted to "eat out" is to make sure that your lover is well-fed and happy at home. We have discovered that the secret to sexual nourishment and total sexual health is a balanced, but varied sexual diet—along with plenty of sexercise!

You may disagree, and that is your right. But if you do, please stop reading *now*.

We have done everything in our power to keep from offending you. You have been fairly warned. From this point forward, you proceed at your own risk.

Why are we so emphatic about this? First, because we care about you. Your sexuality is too important, too precious to be disturbed by a couple of well-meaning authors whose innocent sense of freedom in these matters violates the boundaries you have established as your own.

But the other reason is personal. There is something about criticism in sexual matters that cuts more deeply than words can express. We want so much to help you in this area of vital importance to your marital well-being. But as we have learned the hard way, our risk in doing so is truly great. We have been hurt deeply before.

Consequently, we have worked diligently to use sensitive, appropriate language in the pages that follow. Because you are lovers, we think most of you will feel quite comfortable with the approach we have taken, and will be grateful that we have chosen wording that is sufficiently explicit to be clear. In fact, we are aware that some of you will be disappointed because we have chosen not to go farther. Your personal freedom is such that you will wonder, "Why are they making such a big deal out of this kindergarten stuff?"

But for others of you, what we are about to share will seem to be beyond the college graduate level. In fact, you will fervently insist that it has no place anywhere in the curriculum!

If that is how all of this strikes you, let us once again emphasize that Judy and I deeply respect your position. We have many dear Christian friends who feel as you do, and we love them with all our hearts. Though they and we are aware that God has granted each of us a different level of freedom in this area, we do not allow it to hinder the closeness of our fellowship.

We do not attempt to force our views upon them, nor do they cast aspersions on us. Rather, we share a mutually profound appreciation for the amazing variety God permits within biblical guidelines. None of us feel that our marriage is superior to that of the others. Nor do we privately assume a "holier than thou" attitude behind the others' backs. We are instead humbled by our awareness that God, in His incomprehensible wisdom, made us all so beautifully different.

Rejoice with us then in the unlimited creativity of our God. Some of us may be personally repulsed by the idea of sampling anchovy pizza, rattlesnake meat, pickled pigs' feet, chocolate-covered ants, fried grasshoppers, escargot (snails), peanut-butter-and-mayonnaise sandwiches, watermelon ice cream, or raw Blue Point oysters on the half-shell. But for others among us, these are nothing less than highly prized delicacies!

Frankly, I cannot bear the idea of walking up to a tank in a seafood restaurant and pointing out to my server which living lobster I would like him to kill and put on my plate for me to cut open, chew, and swallow a few minutes later. I am afraid that helpless lobster's scared, beady little eyes would haunt me ever after. The very idea makes my stomach churn.

But I am perfectly willing to grant my dinner companion the freedom to enjoy lobster tail while I stick to more mundane fare. Why? Because God three times commanded Peter, "Do not call anything impure that God has made clean."[1] Peter's shocking vision on that day deeply disturbed traditional Jewish sensibilities. But that scriptural passage reminds me of more than a change of mere dietary restrictions and the inclusion of Gentiles in the fledgling church. On a much larger scale, it reminds me of the enormous freedom introduced by God in the New Testament. It also reminds me that I must not judge everyone according to my own tastes and preferences. God is so much bigger than any of us could ever give Him credit for.

May the uniqueness of our own personal vision never restrict the freedom of others to gratefully and with thanksgiving partake of "delicacies" God has set before them but not before us.

The rest of this book may list some items on the menu that are not in the least appealing to you. That's all right! As your "chefs," we are aware that you will decline to sample some of our "dishes," preferring others instead.

But that is as it should be. Since we are "cooking" for thousands of people with widely differing tastes, all we ask is that the variety of our menu serve as a blessing to you, and that you allow us to also be a blessing to others, where tastes may differ markedly from your own.

How Far Can You Push It?

A s lovers, you already have a healthy sex life. But from time to time you cannot help wondering, "How much better could it be?"

The answer is "There are no limits." Honestly! God has so designed our minds and bodies that we will run out of years on this earth before we run out of things to try to make those years taste even sweeter.

When I was a teenager, an older acquaintance of mine got married. Some time later, I overheard him telling some of the guys at work, "Nah, sex isn't all that great. After the first couple of months, the newness wears off and it's just something else you can do to pass the time, you know?"

As a virgin, I was devastated. Here I had been exercising phenomenal self-control and taken all those cold showers— and for what? For yawning boredom in two short months?

No way, I told myself. That is not going to happen to me. What a put-down of his wife. And what a terrible admission to his own lack of creativity! I resolved then and there that once married, I would personally see to it that my love life would stay vital, exciting, and ever-new.

God is greatly pleased with us when we exercise our

stewardship responsibilities by offering back to Him more than we started with. Is not that the whole point of Jesus' parable of the talents?

To the servants who doubled what their master originally gave them, their master replied, "Well done, good and faithful servant! You have been faithful with a few things; I will put you in charge of many things. Come and share your master's happiness!"[1]

Tragically, however, to the servant who did nothing but preserve his master's gift came the angry reply, "You wicked, lazy servant!"[2]

Is it only with money that God is concerned?[3] Does this parable not teach us God's principles of stewardship for every gift He has so freely bestowed upon us? Does this not include the gift of music, the gift of farming, the gift of speaking, the gift of carpentry . . . and the gift of marital love?

As we can see from this parable, God has not given all of us the same "talents"—whether in music or in lovemaking. To some of us He has given five talents, to others of us He has given two, and to still others, He has given one— each, the Scripture tells us, "according to his ability."[4]

Therefore, when we ask concerning marital love, "How far can you push it?" we are not referring to some predetermined standard against which every couple must be measured. It is not the quantity of return on which God focuses, for no one starts with the same amount. Rather, God wants to know what you did with what you got! It is fascinating to note that He responded with the exact same words of exuberant praise to the servant who brought back four talents, as he did to the one who brought back ten. Why? Because each had developed and increased his talents by exactly the same percentage!

It is not necessary or even relevant, therefore, that you and your spouse make love as frequently or as creatively as any other couple on the face of the earth. Instead, God will be pleased and glorified when the two of you, in utter gratitude to Him, offer the very best you have to give to each other...and to Him.

Once again we ask: "How far can you push it?" In some parts of the world today, people who harvest 60 bushels of corn per acre are considered to be excellent farmers. But in Midwest America, where the climate for growing corn is excellent and the latest hybrids are available, a farmer who brings in only 90 to 100 bushels per acre feels he has had a bad year. In a good year, knowledgeable farmers expect to average 150 bushels per acre—nearly triple what farmers in other parts of the world who have less to work with are able to harvest!

So how much do you have to work with? What are you capable of offering to God, in all areas of your life—including your lovemaking? How many "bushels of love" do you and your spouse have the ability to tenderly present to each other, if you create the right climate, really do your homework, and are willing to experiment freely until you reach your "maximum yield"?

Your answer will be different from that of every other couple who reads this book. But if you give each other and God your very best, you can confidently leave the "harvest" in His hands.

Certainly, there are times even in the very best of marriages when the bells merely tinkle instead of resound with a head-rattling "Bong!" Those times are part of the normal ebb and flow, and should be no cause for alarm. In fact, there is a very definite place in the healthy marriage for "peaceful" lovemaking that is high in tender affection and low in intensity. Keep in mind, too, that what may feel like low tide to you may be high tide for your very different spouse! Low tide is a desirable, normal part of life. If the tide stays out too long for you, however, then it may be time to jump into the water and stir things up!

And that's what this section is all about. What can you do to put some "Zip!" "Zing!" "Zang!" into your love life? How far can you really push it?

Some people take exception to my claim that there are no limits. "The only place you will find cage-rattling, mind-blowing sex is in the movies, in romantic novels, and in pornography," they insist. "Reality is never that good. You do people an injustice if you suggest that such experiences are regularly—or even occasionally—within their reach.

"Why set them up for bitter disappointment? When they discover that they can never quite scale the heights you describe, they blame each other and begin to wonder if they should have married someone else."

But do you know what I take exception to? I take exception to the very idea that Hollywood's glitz or the gutter's sleaze can surpass the wonder God created. The genuine is always superior to the counterfeit. Frankly, I find such defeatist thinking blasphemous. It is appalling to me to hear someone suggest that an unregenerate mind could ever surpass that of Almighty God.

God designed nothing on the cheap. Those who preach the doctrine of low sex expectations reveal the blandness of their own love lives and absolutely nothing of the amazing potential God has built into the two of you as lovers.

If, in spite of your strong desire, you have yet to experience your first eye-crossing tête-à-tête, it's not your fault, it's not your lover's fault, and it is most certainly not God's fault. All you need are some guidelines and the willingness to step out in faith.

We promise you—it's not too late to give your wife thrills, instead of chills. You can still become the woman of your husband's dreams, rather than his screams!

If that is your heart's desire, please read on.

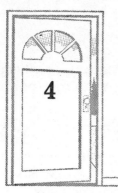

But What Are the Rules?

==#==

Has God established sexual boundaries for a married couple? You'd better believe He has. According to the Bible, then, what are the forbidden behaviors that will harm your sex life?

1. Sexual immorality
2. Impurity
3. Debauchery
4. Orgies
5. Sex with a prostitute
6. Sex with someone to whom you are not married
7. Sex with an animal
8. Heathenistic lust
9. Sex worship
10. Obscenity
11. Coarse joking
12. Homosexuality
13. Mental adultery[1]

Let's take each in turn. Paul clearly defines "sexual immorality" as sex outside of marriage. This includes sex with a prostitute (number 5), sex with someone to whom you are not married (number 6), sex with an animal (number 7), or homosexuality (number 12).

"Impurity" simply means that married sex should not be tainted by references to or participation in sex outside of marriage. For example, if during sex with your spouse you endeavored to increase your excitement by discussing what it would be like to have sex with someone else, you would have introduced an element of "impurity" into your relationship.

"Debauchery" is another way of saying "sexual immorality," only carried to gross extremes, almost with a hint of near insanity.

Another term for "orgies" is "group sex." People at an orgy often pair off with one another's spouses, or sometimes participate in a sexual free-for-all, engaging in various heterosexual and homosexual acts in full view of the others present.

"Heathenistic lust" does not refer to the powerful, God-given sexual desire for each other enjoyed by a married man and woman. Rather, it refers to an unrestrained, indiscriminate sexual desire for men or women other than the person's spouse.

"Sex worship" is idolatry. As wonderful as sex is, it must never take the place of the one who invented it. God alone deserves first place in our lives. A married couple who consistently skipped church to stay home and make love, for example, would fall into this category.

"Obscenity" refers to behavior or language that violates God's requirement to keep sex within the context of marriage. A playful reference to your mate's sexual organs (just between the two of you) would not, for example, be "obscene," since God's ideal is that there be no shame associated with marital nudity.[2] An actor who exhibits his nude body while portraying an adulterous relationship, would, however, fit the biblical definition of "obscenity."

"Coarse joking" does not rule out a sense of sexual humor in marriage. What it rules out is funny stories and scatological quips that refer to sexual sin. "The one about the traveling salesman and the farmer's daughter" should not be listened to, nor repeated.

To excite yourself by imagining what it would be like to have sex with someone other than your mate is to commit "mental adultery." It is dangerous to the health of your marriage, since a mental step toward someone else is a mental step away from your own mate. Some so-called "experts" recommend "harmless" fantasies about other people as a way to liven up marital sex. But consider it for a moment. That is just another way of looking your mate straight in the eye and saying, "You are not exciting enough for me."

Do these rules sound restrictive to you? Do they make you feel as though God wants to deny you significant sexual pleasure? That is not at all what is going on. It isn't that God doesn't want you to enjoy running uninhibitedly through verdant meadows of exciting sexuality. He is just doing you the favor of telling you where the land mines are buried!

There is something about having your right leg blown off that ends up interfering with your joy of running. And there is something about the 13 behaviors mentioned above (and others like them) that eventually destroys what God intended for good *and* your ability to enjoy God's gift of sex to its fullest extent. The Inventor of sex is saying: "These 13 areas are booby traps. They look good, but they can hurt you severely for a long, long time." To ignore God's loving warnings is to risk spending the rest of your life in a sexual "wheelchair."

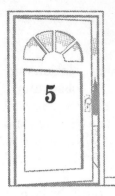

What's Left? God's Very Best!

5

Drink water from your own cistern,
    running water from your own well.
Should your springs overflow in the streets,
    your streams of water in the public squares?
Let them be yours alone,
    never to be shared with strangers.
May your fountain be blessed,
    and may you rejoice in the wife of your youth.
A loving doe, a graceful deer—
    may her breasts satisfy you always,
    may you ever be captivated by her love.[1]

*T*here's no mistaking the exuberant, all-out excitement God intends for marital love in the above passage, is there? "Rejoice" in your mate! That word "rejoice" is not some little spin-your-finger-in-the-air with a bored "whoopee," either. It comes closer to jump-for-the-sky and yell "Waaahoo!"

Solomon also urges you to draw constant "satisfaction" from your lover's charms. The word "satisfaction" denotes

144

the deep, down-to-the-marrow-of-the-bones bubbling joy that comes from happily exhausted satiation.

Don't you dare permit a take-it-or-leave-it attitude toward sex with your mate either, warns Solomon. Instead, allow yourself to be totally head-over-heels "captivated" by the love of your spouse! The feel, here, is that you can't get enough of her ... you are absolutely hooked on him ... your thoughts constantly return to her ... you are mesmerized by the incredible variety, quality, and intensity of his love—but you're not complaining!

That's what obeying God's rules does for you. By removing the weight and danger of sexual sin, you are now free to fly. Trusting obedience frees you to experience the full, explosive measure of what God had in mind when He invented sexual loving.

Listen to the lovemaking rapture God allows to be modeled for you within the pages of sacred Scripture:

Your lovemaking sessions can be intoxicating.

> Let him kiss me with the kisses of his mouth—
> for your love is more delightful than wine.[2]

It's all right to get so carried away that you swoon.

> Strengthen me with raisins,
> refresh me with apples,
> for I am faint with love.[3]

It is completely permissible to become so enamored with each other that you want to make love all night long.

> My lover is mine and I am his;
> he browses among the lilies.

145

Until the day breaks
   and the shadows flee,
turn, my lover,
   and be like a gazelle
or like a young stag
   on the rugged hills.[4]

And whatever you do, don't keep your powerful emotions to yourself! With beautiful, graphic clarity, tell your lover exactly what you intend to do.

Your stature is like that of the palm,
   and your breasts like clusters of fruit.
I said, "I will climb the palm tree;
   I will take hold of its fruit."
May your breasts be like the clusters of the vine,
   the fragrance of your breath like apples,
   and your mouth like the best wine.
May the wine go straight to my lover,
   flowing gently over his lips and teeth.
I belong to my lover,
   and his desire is for me.[5]

Does this sound absolutely glorious, or what? For an even more compelling picture of what God has in store for a husband and wife who long to lose themselves in one another, read the entire Bible book of Songs of Songs. Once you begin to figure out the poetic "code" of Solomon's imagery, all you will be able to say is, "Wow! When does this kind of lovemaking start?"

The answer is "It can start anytime you are ready." As a matter of fact, it could have started long before now. And that is when reality comes crashing in.

"Why Have We Missed Out?"

6

W hy haven't we experienced anything like this up to now?" you would like to know.

Well, it could be that you haven't been married long enough.

"We've been married five years!"

Oh. Then it could be that neither of you desires this level of intensity in sexual loving.

"That's simply not true! We've longed for the kind of relationship the Bible depicts in Song of Songs, but it has always eluded us, no matter how hard we've tried!"

Have you seen a counselor?

"Yes, we spoke to our pastor, but he seemed uncomfortable discussing it with us. So he referred us to a Christian counselor. That was fine with us, but the counselor told us that our sexual expectations were too high. He recommended that we come down to earth and start living in the real world. He ended up chiding us for seemingly not having something more 'productive' to do with our time together as a couple!"

Did you try educating yourselves by reading books on the subject?

"Yes! But that was totally frustrating. Several of the books I brought home were so full of obviously sinful advice that we weren't sure which of the ideas they suggested were actually within the realm of legitimate Christian exploration. So we made the decision to stay with sexual literature that was exclusively Christian."

And?

"In some ways, that was even worse! Maybe our bookstore was out of the best books at the time, but the ones we could find remained at roughly the same level of information as our high school sex education course! Oh, we found a couple of books that seemed to exhibit a healthy attitude toward sex, but just when it seemed they were going to give us the specific counsel we needed, they stopped.

"It was almost like they had arrived at an invisible barrier set by their opinion of what might upset 80-year-old Sister Sophie. So we were left hanging. 'Enjoy God's provision!' they said. But beyond Anatomy 101 and a few very basic guidelines, they never told us *how*!

"What's going on here? Why are Christians afraid to help their fellow Christians experience the sexual ecstasy God clearly blesses in His Word? Why should we be driven to secular books to discover creative sexual strategies? Are Christians that ignorant of their sexual potential? Is Christian sex really that dull?

"It's a strange thing. On every other subject, Christian literature is incredibly detailed—sometimes to a fault. Hundreds of books are written to explore every conceivable aspect of doctrines that, in some cases, may be mentioned in only half a dozen verses in the entire Bible.

"But where is that wholehearted devotion to the 'doctrine' of married sexual happiness? God thought it was so important that in Scripture, He gave it an entire book! Where are all the Christian authors who have made it their business to find out everything God has for His people sexually? And why are they unwilling to go over every aspect of the subject with a fine-tooth comb, like they do on everything else?

"We Christians say we believe married sex is holy, and that it was created by God. But when we go to Christian 'experts' for advice, some of them act as though we have no right to desire all God has for us in this area of our lives!"

Amen. That's good preaching. We have an answer for you, but it's not nearly as good as your questions.

In all fairness to Christian counselors, the typical session consists of a male counselor and a female client whose husband refuses to come in for marital therapy. Under those conditions, a wise counselor is simply not going to go into intimate detail. Those who do usually live to regret it.

All too often, even when the husband is present, he is there reluctantly. Some time you ought to try to bring up a delicate subject like sex with a defensive man who thinks you are questioning his masculinity! You will quickly discover that you are wasting your time. Only in a nonthreatening atmosphere can real progress be made in such a sensitive area.

When the rare couple like you comes along, therefore, the counselor is totally unprepared. His orientation is toward sickness rather than wellness. Most of the troubled people who come to see him would be thrilled if they were able to achieve your current level of sexual function—and so, frankly, would he! In effect, you have arrived in his office dissatisfied with the kind of sex life that he regards as the goal!

In the case of most Christian counselors, little or nothing in his professional training has prepared him for your questions. Sadly, it may be that nothing in his personal life has prepared him for your questions, either. So, embarrassed over his lack of expertise, he does the human thing and transfers the blame to you for bringing up the subject in the first place!

Qualified Christian authors have their obstacles to overcome, too. Even if they are willing to risk the personal attack that is likely to come from their less-tolerant "brothers and sisters," they may not be able to find anyone willing to publish their book. Secular publishers don't like all the scriptural references, and they flatly disagree with the biblical prohibitions. Christian publishers are fearful that bookstores will refuse to carry the book, or that inhibited Christian readers will be too embarrassed to pick it up off the shelf, carry it up to the cash register, and buy it—no matter how desperately they want to read it!

So, as you can easily see, what you now hold in your hands is a rare book. Is the climate right? Are Christians ready? Or will we receive a hail of gunfire that comes not from our enemies but from our "friends"?

For these reasons, Judy and I have barely scratched the surface in this book of what God has taught us about the potential that exists in Christian marriage. Of course, it is only prudent to be guided by what is publishable, rather than by sharing everything you may wish to know.

Even so, what you are about to read breaks new ground. If you are grateful, and if you believe that the publishing of this book is Christ-honoring, please let us know. Believe me, those who strongly disagree certainly will.

God's Gift to His People: "Clean Zing!"

*I*t is for freedom that Christ has set us free. Stand firm, then, and do not let yourselves be burdened again by a yoke of slavery."[1]

After making that declaration to the Galatian church, Paul applied it to the doctrinal error of some who taught circumcision as a prerequisite to salvation. But is it only from works heresies that Christ has freed us?

"I have come that they may have life," Jesus boldly proclaimed in the very presence of His enemies, "and have it to the full."[2]

Is not godly marital joy a part of the "full life" Jesus graciously grants to His devoted married followers? Or do we, like the ascetics, attempt to confine our perception of God's bounty to solely cerebral pursuits?

No! A thousand times no! The same God who made our minds, souls, and spirits also made our bodies[3] and gave them the full range of expression—including our sexuality[4]—to enjoy.

Did Satan create the rapturous transport of married lovemaking? Is he the one a wife should thank when her husband's skillful caresses bring her to the peak of ecstasy?

Does the devil deserve a husband's gratitude as wave after wave of indescribable pleasure sweep over him in the arms of his loving wife? God forbid!

> Don't be deceived, my dear brothers. Every good and perfect gift is from above, coming down from the Father of the heavenly lights, who does not change like shifting shadows.[5]

Is God concerned only with the intellectual pursuits of marriage, choosing to ignore the bodies He Himself created, as though they were somehow beneath the dignity of His lavish blessing? No, praise His wonderful name, He does not. He is delighted with His entire creation[6] and expects us, as stewards of all He has created, to explore, discover, fulfill, and rule over the potential He has placed within us.[7]

"Husbands ought to love their wives as their own *bodies*," Paul teaches. "He who loves his wife loves himself. After all, no one ever hated his own body"![8]

How healthy are the words of Scripture for all who have eyes to see and ears to hear. God isn't mad at us for having bodies—he's the one who gave them to us! God isn't displeased with our constant pursuit of new ways to bring pleasure and delight to our spouses—He's the one who granted us the ability and the creativity to do that very thing!

Are you thankful for God's gracious "wedding gift" to you? Are you truly grateful that He did not confine you to mere words as you seek to fully express your deep love for one another? We "old-fashioned Christians" are extremely meticulous about saying grace before meals. But I wonder—have you ever paused to give thanks to God before, during, or after a marvelous session of lovemaking?[9]

Judy and I have, many times. Before you dismiss such gratitude to God as a bit peculiar, ask yourself this question: For which are you actually more thankful: a forkful of beans, or your lover's kiss? Of the two, which is the more sophisticated? Which exhibits God's greater artistry? For that matter, if you were forced to choose, which would you rather do without?

> Oh, the depth of the riches of the
>   wisdom and knowledge of God!
> How unsearchable his judgments,
>   and his paths beyond tracing out!
> "Who has known the mind of the Lord?
>   Or who has been his counselor?"
> "Who has ever given to God,
>   that God should repay him?"
> For from him and through him and
>   to him are all things.
> To him be the glory forever!
>   Amen.[10]

In light of the awesome majesty of our God, why should we reduce such brilliance to the wattage of a dimly lit lamp? Is God glorified when we make His greatness small or when we diminish the potential of any part of His creation? How is it pleasing to the Lord when we place upon ourselves limitations in any area—including marital love—that God Himself does not place on us?

Nowhere in Scripture do we find taught such a strange, restrictive philosophy. Rather, Paul instructs Timothy to command even those who are wealthy "to put their hope in God, who richly provides us with *everything* for our *enjoyment*."[11]

Who says God's commands are burdensome!

Simply put, if God doesn't prohibit a particular sexual practice, why should we? Jesus had strong words for religious teachers who load up people with rules and regulations that God never gave, so as to rob them of their freedom in Christ.

Isaiah was right when he prophesied about
you hypocrites; as it is written:

"These people honor me with their
lips,
but their hearts are far from me.
They worship me in vain;
their teachings are but rules
taught by men."

You have let go of the commands of God and
are holding on to the traditions of men.[12]

If you read the Bible from cover to cover, you will be amazed to discover that, basically speaking, all of God's rules for married sexual behavior may be summed up in a single sentence: *You may do anything you wish, so long as it harms neither of you and involves no one else.*

"But," you may wonder, "doesn't that open things up to some pretty...well...amazing practices?"

Precisely.

"But...but...how can that be Christian?"

We have an "amazing" God!

"Granted—it's just that I can't help questioning whether God wants a married couple to become all that carried away with each other. Galatians 5:24 does say we are supposed to have crucified our passions and desires, you know."

Well, that's close, but it's not exactly what it says. Let's take a closer look: "Those who belong to Christ Jesus have crucified the sinful nature with its passions and desires."[13]

"But isn't that what I just said?"

No, although it is easy to miss the distinction upon first reading. Galatians 5:24 does *not* say Christians have crucified their passions and desires. God does not intend for Christians to be passionless and desireless. That is the avowed objective of Buddhism, not Christianity. Such a philosophy is far more compatible with Eastern cultism than it is with biblical truth. Instead, Galatians 5:24 says Christians have crucified the passions and desires of *the sinful nature*!

"I guess I just don't see the difference between the two."

You're right, it is a little difficult to discuss abstractly. Let's take an example: The sinful nature might make you desire a man who is not your husband, and eventually burn with passion for him. Since you belong to Christ, however, you have crucified those passions and desires and must therefore refuse to give in to them.

"I'm with you so far."

Ah, but the very thing that would be wrong for you to feel toward another man is, in fact, God's plan for you to feel toward your husband. God *wants* a woman to desire her husband!

"Forgive me," you may rightfully ask, "but do you have any Scripture to back that up?"

How about Genesis 3:16?

"Which says?"

Which says, quoting God in His commandment to Eve, the first woman He created: "Your desire will be for your husband."[14]

"All right," you concede, "I guess I'll have to accept that. But wait a minute! Didn't God make that pronouncement right after she had sinned?"

Yes, He did.

"Well, there you have it. Desire is a punishment, reserved for the ungodly and disobedient."

I don't blame you for considering that possibility. But that's why I'm thankful for Psalm 20:4.

"I don't believe I'm familiar with that verse."

It's a good one! The first five verses of the twentieth psalm record a prayer of blessing to be bestowed by God upon the righteous. Then David proclaims, "May he give you the desire of your heart."[15]

"All right, you've made your point! There is a place for 'desire' in holy marriages. But it certainly didn't say a woman had to be 'passionate' about her desire for her husband."

You're right. That issue was covered in blanket fashion by Solomon, David's son.

"And where did he say that?"

It's recorded in the Book of Ecclesiastes, chapter nine, verse ten: "Whatever your hand finds to do, do it with all your might."

In this verse, Solomon reveals the exuberance with which God expects us to approach life. He is offended by halfhearted, halfway, listless, passionless living...and loving!

"God wants us to go all out?"

All out.

"No barriers?"

None, except those set by God.

"How did you word that again?"

You may do anything you wish, so long as it harms neither of you and involves no one else.

"Clean 'zing!' huh?"
Clean "zing"!
"This is very freeing."
That's exactly what Christianity is supposed to do.

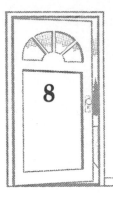

Why Did You Get Married, After All?

"W hy did you get married?"

I've asked a lot of people that question, but I have yet to hear anyone reply, "Because, among other things, we wanted to express our love through the intimacy of sex!"

As brazen as that may sound, if a couple ever did offer that reason, they would be giving a scriptural reply! Paul instructed the church at Corinth,

> It is good for a man not to marry. But since there is so much immorality, each man should have his own wife, and each woman her own husband.[1]

Referring to sex, Paul goes on to say,

> The husband should fulfill his marital duty to his wife, and likewise the wife to her husband. The wife's body does not belong to her alone but also to her husband. In the same way, the husband's body does not belong to him alone but also to his wife.[2]

Furthermore, he instructs them,

> Do not deprive each other except by mutual
> consent and for a time, so that you may devote
> yourselves to prayer. Then come together
> again so that Satan will not tempt you
> because of your lack of self-control.[3]

Nowhere else in this self-centered age will you find
anything approaching the total sexual access to one another that is granted to a husband and wife by God Himself.
When a wife says to her husband, "Darling, please make
love to me," God does not give the husband the option of
ignoring her needs continually by replying, "Not now. I'm
busy."

When a husband says to his wife, "Sweetheart, I really
need you," God does not give her the option of constantly
putting him off with, "Sorry, I'm just not in the mood."

It would be a mistake, however, to suppose that with the
granting of such complete rights to each other's bodies,
God does not include balancing guidelines. Throughout
the Bible, God commands His people to give high priority
to the needs of others:

> Do nothing out of selfish ambition or vain
> conceit, but in humility consider others better
> than yourselves. Each of you should look not
> only to your own interests, but also to the
> interests of others.[4]

The same God who instructed, "Wives, in the same way
be submissive to your husbands," also commanded, "Husbands in the same way be considerate as you live with your

wives."[5] Therefore, as a loving husband you will be exceedingly sensitive to your wife's personal timing, her needs, her stressors, her preferences—and yes, to her moods. Certainly you have a God-given right to satisfy your sexual needs in the arms of your wife. But love demands that you consider her needs even ahead of your own.

Certainly it is wrong, and even dangerous, for a man to go to bed night after night frustrated and unfulfilled because his wife has "another headache." But it is just as wrong and dangerous for a man to force himself upon his wife without regard for her feelings or physical condition just because he "has the urge."

The Bible's emphasis is not upon claiming our rights in marriage but upon meeting one another's needs. Suppose your husband comes home dead-tired, but all day long you have yearned to feel him inside you and to lose yourself in the total release of loving physical union. You could deprive yourself and say nothing, or you could give in to your strong desire and demand that he make passionate love to you, in spite of his weary state.

But there is another option available. Why not say to him, "Darling, I've thought about having you all day, but I can see that you are exhausted. So why don't you lie back tonight and let me make love to you? Just relax and let me do all the work." Rough though his day may have been, you have just made your husband an offer that he probably can't refuse!

As you can easily see, such an adjustment allows you to enjoy your marital privileges, while simultaneously showing genuine sensitivity to your husband's low energy level. In this case, we don't have a winner and a loser. Instead, loving consideration has motivated you to come up with a solution that is win-win.

Paul goes on to explain that the single life is a great life for those who have the God-given ability to remain celibate without temptation. "But if they cannot control themselves," Paul concludes, "they should marry, for it is better to marry than to burn with passion."[6]

There you have it—bold, bright, and healthy as daylight. The Bible specifically tells you that the gift of sexual fulfillment is one of the reasons he brings a man and woman together in holy wedlock! Furthermore, Paul makes it clear that sex is not some side issue in marriage to be worked in if there is time, but only after everything else is taken care of. On the contrary, he places it right alongside companionship and procreation as a legitimate motivation for Christians to marry.

But let's see why. In the Scripture verses immediately preceding the passage we've just looked at, Paul forbids sexual union with a prostitute. Then he warns,

> Flee from sexual immorality. All other sins
> a man commits are outside his body, but he
> who sins sexually sins against his own body.
> Do you not know that your body is a temple of
> the Holy Spirit, who is in you, whom you have
> received from God? You are not your own; you
> were bought at a price. Therefore honor God
> with your body.[7]

Obviously, then, a second purpose for married sex is to keep you from wanting to have sex with someone else. "Since there is so much immorality," he counsels, "each man should have his own wife, and each woman her own husband."[8]

But let me ask you a question: Will just *any* old kind of married sex keep you from wanting someone else? Certainly something is better than nothing! But the truth is, there is a much better way to keep yourself from being tempted. And that is to make sure that what you have is *better* than the temptation that is being waved under your nose!

Or put another way: Does dull, unimaginative, uninspired, same-old-thing sex protect a married person from Satan's temptation? Suppose you're sitting in a restaurant, trying to eat only healthy foods, and the person next to you is digging in to a fat, juicy, thickly marbled steak. If all you have on your plate is a sad, limp little piece of stringy, bitter-tasting celery, it's going to be awfully hard to resist temptation. You're going to feel sorry for yourself and feel like ordering yourself a nice, big, fat, juicy steak, too!

But what if your server places before you a huge, colorful chef's salad, complete with a dozen different fresh, crisp vegetables, all topped off with lean strips of turkey and a rich, tangy, low-cal dressing? Why, your "steak temptation" is going to wither away to nothing!

Your dinner companions will take one look at your massive, artistically prepared salad and say, "Wow!"

Mouth watering in anticipation, you'll say to yourself, "Good grief! There's no way I'm going to be able to eat all of this!"

And what about the guy sitting next to you with that fat steak in front of him? He's probably muttering to himself, "Great. She gets to eat that delicious, beautifully prepared salad, lose weight, and feel great. Meanwhile, I'm paying twice as much for this steak, which is going to make me fatter, clog my arteries, and cause me to feel sluggish for the rest of the evening."

So who is going to end up feeling jealous of whom? Right.

And that's what the rest of this book is all about. To borrow a slogan, we're going to show you how to enjoy "all of the pleasure, with none of the guilt."

We are about to spread before you a rather exciting array of legitimate sexual options for Christian marriage. You may be enamored with everything you see. In that case, help yourself!

On the other hand, if we serve up your chef's salad with a vegetable that is a little too exotic for your taste, don't let it bother you for a single moment. Simply lift it off with your fork, lay it aside...and enjoy the rest.

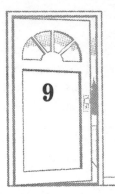

9

You Gotta Learn to Let Go!

I f you have never yet experienced mind-boggling love-making with your spouse, it is unlikely that the problem can be traced to your ignorance of male/female anatomy. As lovers, you may have read a half-dozen or more books that illustrated scores of acrobatic positions, explained just how to find the G-spot, extolled the benefits of ESO (Extended Sexual Orgasm), and interpreted the latest findings from Masters and Johnson.

No doubt it is frustrating to you to discover that all this knowledge still isn't enough to lift you to the level of ecstasy that you instinctively know is there, just waiting for you. But listen very carefully: Your problem is more likely one of *timidity* than it is of *technique*.

"Me? Timid? Oh, come on!" you may protest. "You wouldn't say that if you knew me!"

And perhaps I wouldn't. But remember what level we are on here. College football players think they know what hard hitting is, until they enter the pros. Minor league batters think they know what a fastball is until they step up to the plate in the majors. Compared to anyone or anything else you know, you may be one liberated lover.

But the moment you picked up this book, you signaled your intention to enter another league.

So I'll say it again: If you have yet to hit the ball out of the park in your lovemaking, you are probably checking your swing. Perhaps even without knowing it, you are holding something back. And that something can make all the difference between a high fly ball that is caught against the wall and one that sails over into the stands for a home run.

How can that happen? Your sexuality is, arguably, the most private part of your life. Since you have already opened that part of your life to your spouse, you can't be blamed for protesting, "I've already done that! What else is there?" But your sexuality itself has within it many dimensions. Some of those dimensions are more private than others—and therefore harder to share, even with your mate.

It's a little like inviting someone into the foyer of your home. When you allow him to cross your threshold, you have made a big distinction between him and the rest of the outside world. But your house has many rooms. How far will you allow him to enter? Will you stop him at the living room/guest bathroom area? Or will you allow him to step into your kitchen...to see your den...to use the master bath?

But there is still another dimension. Are you willing to go on vacation and leave him alone for a week while he pokes around in every nook and cranny of your house? Or better yet, will you personally take him into your basement, your attic, and your closets? Will you show him where you've hidden your safe, give him the combination, and invite him to help himself to its contents anytime he pleases?

To say, "Of course I've invited Jack into my home!" doesn't tell me very much, does it? The real question is "Just how *far* did you let Jack in?"

And so it is with your sexuality. As strange as it may sound, it is entirely possible—comparatively speaking, now—to have fairly impersonal sex. You can allow your husband to enter your body night after night without ever permitting him to go beyond the "living room/guest bathroom" area.

When he leaves for work in the morning, he may mistakenly think he has seen your whole "house." But what is just as common among lovers, you may actually believe that you have opened yourself up as far as another human being is ever supposed to enter! It's not that you have refused him entry to your "kitchen," your "den," your "bedroom," your "attic," or your "safe"—it's just that the thought has never even crossed your mind!

Subconsciously, you may have lived your entire life assuming that nobody could, would, or should hold a one-person sexual "open house"! In fact, even as I mention it, the possibility may frighten you a little—or a lot.

"What are the limits here?" you may wonder.

None but God's.

"But... where does that mean my husband might go?"

Anywhere he pleases.

"Yes, but what do you think he will—you know—*do*?"

Whatever he wants.

"Ah, well, you see, I have this one area that I really never—"

That's probably the very first place he will want to explore—in depth... at length... under the lights.

"Hmmmm. Frankly, this sounds a little risky."

No, it isn't just a "little" risky. It's downright dangerous. It is dangerous to the privacy you have always maintained as your own person. It is dangerous to your current self-concept. It is dangerous to the neat little box in which you now keep your idea of who your husband actually is. It is dangerous to the set of unspoken rules by which you now operate. In short, it is dangerous to the status quo of your entire marriage.

And it is most definitely not for everybody. Maybe you should put this book down now and go for a walk. Since you know God, this would be a good time to do some praying. Or if you don't know God as well as you might, this wouldn't be a bad time to start getting better acquainted. Because where you are considering going, you're gonna need Him.

After your walk, you may come back and throw this book away. And that's all right. You've already got your money's worth because you have discovered how far you want to go—and how far you do *not* want to go—in your marriage. You are not any less a person nor worse a lover for your decision. Whether they admit it to themselves or not, *all* people have their limits. And you have just bumped into yours.

On the other hand, you may choose to exercise financial prudence and simply put this book high on some dimly lit shelf that doesn't catch your eye too often, allowing it to gather some dust—not a bad idea, actually. Give yourself some time. Don't rush in where angels fear to (well, in this case, "cannot") tread.

What you want to be asking yourself, your spouse, and your God is "What kind of person am I—Superman or Clark Kent? What kind of couple are we? Are we really the banzai specialists that we think we are? Or would we be just as happy toasting marshmallows in front of the fire, instead of igniting an inferno in our bedroom that we may not be able to extinguish before we both get burned?

Nothing's simple, is it? And to compound matters, few things are as complex as your sexuality. We owed you this one last warning. Maybe we owed it to ourselves, too. But enough's enough. We're eager to go on.

And now it's time for you to decide.

10 Let Go of Your Fear of Rejection

═══╬═══

Still here? Great. Or maybe you've just rejoined us after some "shelf time." In that case, blow off the dust and get ready for a real adventure.

Hey, do you know what? The first thing you must do is to let go of your fear of rejection. Non-lovers simply cannot do this because the only love they know is conditional. They don't feel accepted for who they are. They are too nervous about their paunchy stomachs or their flat chests. They cannot completely let go because they believe they will lose what little respect they have: "He'll think I'm ugly!" or "If she sees me like this, she'll laugh!"

But if you and your spouse are truly lovers, a few moments of quiet reflection should remind you that you really know better than that. Lovers accept one another, shortcomings and all. And then they go farther than that. Lovers fall in love with each other's shortcomings.

Confess to your husband your fear of rejection. Tell him you are afraid that he will wince when he sees your appendix scar or be offended by your varicose veins. Then listen to him and believe him when he hushes your concerns by telling you that he loves you just the way you are.

Trust your spouse's love. Let go of your fear of rejection. And then someday, Mr. or Mrs. Shyness, when things are a little slow, you can liven them up just a smidgen by throwing open your bathrobe and saying, "Hey—feast your eyes on *this!*"

Well, maybe not. That only works for certain kinds of personalities.

11

Let Go of Your Inhibitions

Making love in the dark requires you to relax your inhibitions, but not as much as making love by candlelight, which allows your lover to catch dim glimpses of your body. You must relax your inhibitions even more to make love with all the lights on. But to willingly and excitedly assume a dozen different poses so your lover can thoroughly explore every inch of your body means you really have to learn how to let go!

Most of us have heard our "inhibition tape" kick in and start to play its warning message when we accidentally trip its preset limits: "Stop! What do you think you are doing? This is one of those things that simply must not be done!"

The trouble is, your "inhibition tape" sounds so much like your conscience that you are apt to pay attention to its official-sounding bluster and back off. It is vital, therefore, that you clearly distinguish between the two.

Your conscience is your inner alarm that goes off when you are about to do something wrong. You are right, certainly, to avoid at all costs the violation of your God-given conscience. Your "inhibition tape," however, is an arbitrary internal device that you may have last set for yourself in the first grade. The idea was to keep you from doing anything even a little bit different, to prevent your classmates from laughing at you.

Don't you think it's about time that you reset your "inhibition tape"?

Inhibitions are still quite appropriate in other social settings, of course, although you will discover that you would be wise to adopt a different set of rules from the ones you operated under when you were six years old! But inhibitions are as out-of-place for a lover in the bedroom as are a pair of steel-toed work boots on a ballerina dancing *The Nutcracker Suite*. They do tend to trip you up.

The next five doorways give you a look at some of the more common inhibition triggers and expose them for the lovemaking clodhoppers they really are. Enter each doorway with an open mind and a lover's determination to soar higher than ever before as you thrill to the dance of love. Just remember as you step into these next five doorways: If the shoe fits... throw it away!

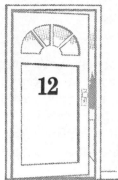

12

Let Go of Your Fear of Ridicule

The first inhibiting factor we'll examine is the fear of ridicule. In some marriages this is a very real concern, but not in yours. The two of you are lovers, remember? Your mate simply is not going to laugh at and make fun of you, the way Tommy Schwartz did that day you ended up with a white mustache because you tipped up the carton and thoroughly enjoyed your milk. Ever since then you have been hesitant to drink deeply of life, for fear it will leave the residue of a faux pas on your gleeful little face.

I've got an assignment for both of you. Go out and buy a couple of milk cartons—the half-pint size you used to get with your lunch at school. Take them home and put them in the refrigerator so they get good and cold. Then, as a prelude to your next lovemaking session, get totally undressed and break out those memory-loaded milk cartons.

Open them up on one end into that nice little diamond-shaped hole—remember? Click your two cartons together in a playful "toast," lift them to your lips, and then simultaneously tilt your heads straight back, bottoms up!

Let the milk pour in an unchecked stream into your throat, out the corners of your mouth, in your ears, around your chin, and down your neck! Enjoy the sweet, cold liquid as it floods your mouth. Don't stop pouring until all of it is either in you or on you. Then, still laughing, choking, and sputtering, embrace one another in a hilarious milky-white-mustache French kiss!

That should loosen you up a bit.

It might also teach you several important lessons. First, it will remind you that there is all the difference in the world in being laughed *at* and being laughed *with*. Secondly, it might occur to you that the only reason Tommy Schwartz ridiculed you way back when is that he didn't know how to enjoy his own milk nearly as much as you did. Finally, and by far most importantly, you will learn that the next time you follow some authors' advice to pour milk all over yourselves, you would be wise to cover your bed with bath towels!

Let Go of Others' Opinions

The second trigger of your inhibitions is your fear of the opinions of others. You cannot relax and enjoy one another sexually so long as you nervously imagine that you are performing before a disapproving audience.

"What would my mother say if she knew what I was doing now?"

With all due respect to your mother, may I help you with the biblical reminder that she would be out-of-place if she said a single word? "For this reason," the Bible states, "a man will leave his father and mother and be united to his wife, and they will become one flesh."[1]

Quite clearly, one of God's purposes in marriage is the birth of a new, autonomous entity. Nobody—God included—ever gave your parents the right to interfere in your married sex life unless you are being abused or have decided to bring in a third party.

Therefore, it really doesn't matter whether or not your mother would be scandalized by the thrilling, "forbidden" things you and your mate enjoy. According to God's infinitely wise plan, those apron strings were supposed to have been clipped when you got married. It sounds, however, as though you may have left a few threads hanging. It is time, therefore, to get out the scissors.

Besides, although you may think you know your mother inside and out, you probably don't know her as well as you imagine you do. Most mothers compartmentalize their lives. They are one person with their children, but quite another person with their husbands. Even those mothers who have disappointing relationships with their husbands may have secret, godly, unfulfilled wishes and desires that—if they could—they would be only too happy to grant to you, for you and your spouse to enjoy.

Many children make the mistake of thinking their parents are old fuddy-duddies who, if they still have any sex life at all, do it in the dark once or twice a year. Likely as not, if the truth were actually known, your parents could probably teach the two of you a thing or two!

"Well, even if I could get past the barrier of my parents' approval, I sincerely doubt that my minister would approve of some of the things my wife wants us to do!"

First of all, you probably have no real knowledge of what your minister would or would not approve. You might be stunned to learn the wide range of sexual freedom he believes the Bible actually permits a husband and wife to enjoy. Just because he cannot stand up in the pulpit on a Sunday morning and read off the whole list does not mean he would disapprove of what you and your wife did Saturday night.

But secondly, so long as you enjoy it and it involves no one else, what your minister thinks about your latest sexual experiment is irrelevant.

"My girlfriends would give me a really hard time if they knew what I was doing for my husband right now."

Perhaps they would. Let's suppose that your girlfriends have compiled a long list of sexual favors that they would never ever be willing to offer to their husbands. Is that something for them to be proud of, or is it a crying, selfish, shortsighted shame?

As a result of their warped sense of feminine "dignity," they are probably married to uptight, unfulfilled men. But your deep love for your husband would never allow him to suffer as their husbands must.

If you have to think such thoughts, go ahead and think them the rest of the way out: "Yes, my girlfriends would give me a hard time if they knew what I am willing to do for my husband. But their husbands would probably give anything if their wives were willing to treat them as well as I enjoy treating my husband!"

Nor are all of your concerns self-imposed. "I've just read a book by an expert I genuinely respect," you may tell me. "He recommends against one of the sexual practices that my spouse and I have enjoyed for years. Should we stop?"

Yes. You should stop allowing so-called "experts" to run your life. When it comes to your marriage, you, your spouse, and God are the only experts, not some author—including the ones you are reading right now.

"Yes, but if anyone ever found out about the kinds of things my wife and I do together, they would just die!"

Then for goodness' sake, spare their lives! Don't tell them! Why should you dangle at the end of a rope tied to somebody else's hang-ups? If they want to choke the life out of their own sexuality, that's their business. But you have no obligation to strangle with them.

Let Go of Your Fear of Embarrassment

14

This is another inhibiting factor that grabbed many of us in its restrictive clutches when we were children. You will always remember the afternoon when your history teacher asked you to read aloud in class. You were a little nervous as you began, but then your voice steadied and things seemed to be going all right—until you heard the first titters of laughter.

You tried to ignore them, hoping against hope that it had nothing to do with you. But every time you read the word "colonel," their snickers grew louder. Your mind raced frantically, silently screaming, "What am I doing wrong? What? What?" as you stumbled through to the end of the passage.

Finally you finished and looked up in bewilderment at your teacher, who was fighting unsuccessfully to keep a big grin off her face. "Thank you," she said. "That was very nice. However, I believe you will find that the word is pronounced 'ker-nal,' rather than 'co-loan-al.'"

At that, the class burst into open laughter, your "friends" shaking their heads and pounding their desks in helpless mirth. You could feel your face flaming beet-red as you somehow made your way back to your chair to the sounds of your classmates chortling, "Co-*loan*-al!" "Co-*loan*-al!"

That night, as you lay in bed unable to sleep, replaying the scene in your mind for the hundredth time, you vowed that you would never allow anything like that to happen to you again. And you haven't. The next time you were called on to read in class, you explained that you had a sore throat. When your best friend urged you to try out for the school play the following year, you declined.

Over the years, your avoidance behavior has become automatic. It is second nature to you to size up the "embarrassment potential" of any activity in about two seconds flat. If there is the slightest possibility that you might be placed in an uncomplimentary light, you shake your head with a tight smile and reply, "No thank you," offering no explanation.

Now you're a grown-up. You're a very good lover, too... up to a point. There isn't a single sexual act you are unwilling to perform for your spouse, and you take considerable pride in that fact. The one thing you cannot bear, however, is when your mate attempts to focus all the attention on you.

You are able to orgasm during lovemaking in the dark, but with the lights on and your husband watching your face... you just can't. Or, you are more than willing to lovingly and skillfully caress your wife at her merest request, but you become much less cooperative when the focus shifts from her to you.

Once, in the first year of your marriage, your husband got carried away, put on some music with a pounding beat, and asked you to dance for him. He obviously had become so enraptured with you that he wanted to fill his eyes with your beauty. But you demurred, once again out of embarrassment.

Your husband was obviously disappointed, but withdrew his request. As you look back you experience a pang of regret because that level of excitement has never come over him again.

Or perhaps your wife once asked you to writer her a love sonnet and read it to her before lovemaking. The very idea of doing that made you blanch. If the guys ever got wind of this. . . . You put her off, explaining that poetry just wasn't your gift.

Don't you see? Because of your needless fear of embarrassment, you have unintentionally put restrictions on your lovemaking that God never commanded. Without really meaning to, you have installed a governor on your mutual excitement for fear your spouse will get carried away and want something else from you that may make you feel uncomfortable. As a result, some of the sexual spontaneity that you and your lover would both dearly enjoy is lost.

The hardest part about all of this is that your embarrassment prevents you from communicating the true depth of your love for your mate. You love your spouse with all your heart, but your embarrassment blocks you from showing that love with all of your body. It has to upset you that other men or women, no less holy than you, who love their spouses even less than you love your dear mate, freely give to their mate all the exciting pleasures that your embarrassment will not permit you to grant to yours.

Just think about it. Unlike so many cheating spouses, yours is faithful to you. Therefore, you are your lover's only hope! You and you alone are the one person in this world who can allow your mate to taste the special delights of married love that should be rightfully his or hers for the asking. Why should your lover do without?

You are your spouse's garden. You abound with petunias, irises, daffodils, violets, begonias. "What else could my lover want?" you ask. "My mate can have all of these flowers he or she wishes, anytime he or she desires!"

But what if your spouse yearns for the delicate fragrance of your deep-red Masterpiece Rose? There it is in your garden—your lover's garden!—tall, robust, and lush, glistening with dewdrops that sparkle invitingly from its tantalizingly open petals. Will you decline to pick it and lovingly offer it to your lover for fear that a thorn of embarrassment might prick your finger?

When you think about it—really think about it...you may decide that there is something far more embarrassing than the actions you have rejected up to now. And that is for you to have to explain why you have chosen to deprive your darling of the intimate delights he or she had every right to expect would be his or hers when your mate forsook all others and took you for a lifetime mate.

"Okay. You've made your point. I'm embarrassed about it already. So how do I go about making amends? How do I let my spouse know I want to make up for lost time?"

Well, you could tell your spouse what you just now told me. I guarantee you that would make your mate's day— and probably week, month, and year! As a surprise you could dig out that old phonograph record he put on during the first year of your marriage, ask him to kindly be seated, and proceed to honor a certain gentleman's request that is decidedly overdue! Or you could start composing that sonnet and practice reading it with tender expression until you are able to deliver it some evening after supper with wife-melting effectiveness.

15

Let Go of Your Fear That You Will Lose Control

——#——

Afourth common inhibitor is your fear that if you totally give in to your feelings, you will lose control.

You may be the kind of person for whom control in every area of your life is highly important. Perhaps, when given a choice, you would rather drive the car than sit on the passenger's side. If you are not the one who handles the finances in your family, you would probably prefer to be. It's not that you have the time to spare or even particularly enjoy paying bills. It's just that you like to know where the money is going and to be sure you are using it as wisely as possible.

Your fear of losing control isn't a sexual issue. It's a personality issue. Being in control is the method your self-preservation instinct has chosen to manifest itself. It's how you keep from getting hurt.

When you are the one behind the wheel of your car, you are able to be certain that your speed is within safe limits, that you are maintaining a proper distance from the car in front of you, and that the brakes are rapidly pumped rather than jammed to the floor when you have to stop on ice or snow. With you in the driver's seat, you know you will never get a ticket and that you are much less likely to be involved in a traffic accident.

When you are the one who handles the finances, you feel more confident that all the bills will be paid on time, that the checkbook balance is current and sufficient, and that the proper amount of money has been set aside for savings. As long as you hold the purse strings, you believe that you will be much more ready to weather any financial emergency that comes along.

Why should you approach sex in any other way? It's how you handle everything else. You like to be in control and to maintain control, no matter what. That's just who you are. So what if you don't like to close your eyes for very long during a kiss? What difference does that make, you'd like to know? So what if you want to know precisely what you and your wife are going to be doing sexually each time before you do it? If you fail to plan, you're planning to fail, right?

You've learned the hard way that you have to be on your guard. You have to watch your back. If you don't, you are convinced bad things can happen—and you are prepared to cite specific examples of just how bad some of those things have turned out to be, for anybody who wants to listen.

If that is true on the highway or when dealing with the bank, then it is doubly true in bed. In some ways, the bedroom is a scary place for you. It is where you close your eyes and become unconscious for up to eight hours at a time, totally unprotected, out of control. Consequently, you frequently have trouble falling asleep—or going back to sleep, should you awaken in the middle of the night.

There is another reason that the bedroom makes you slightly nervous. It is the place where you take off your clothes. As each article of clothing is removed, you become more vulnerable. You're not paranoid about it, of course, but that's why you're a pajama man.

You cannot imagine why anyone would ever sleep in the nude. What if there were a fire during the night? You could lose your life while hunting for something to put on so you could run outside! And what if a thief attempted to break in? How would he be able to take you seriously if he saw you standing there shaking your finger at him and ordering him to leave, without a stitch of clothing on your quavering, defenseless body?

You enjoy sex, sure. But you've had to admit to yourself more than once that it also makes you feel, well, slightly uncomfortable. It's not that you don't love your mate with all your heart—you do! It's just that, as strange as it would sound to ever admit it to anyone, you enjoy having *had* sex more than having it. When it's over, your contented wife lies there, snuggled in your arms, and you both bask in the lazy afterglow. Everything is back under control.

But while you are actually making love, somehow you feel at risk, as though events could take a sudden, unexpected turn and you wouldn't know how to handle them. What are the *rules* for this activity? Where are the boundaries? You want to know when "enough" is enough!

Shortly after your wedding, you went out and bought a marriage manual, in search of a set of guidelines. The author wasn't as specific as you would have liked, but at least you were able to piece together what was supposed to be the typical order of events: foreplay, arousal, intercourse, orgasm, resolution. Great. Five clearly defined steps.

The only trouble is, making love to your wife never worked out in real life the way it was supposed to on paper. You did everything in your power to orchestrate everything perfectly, but you were never quite able to follow the proper procedure. There were just too many variables!

To this very day, you continue to struggle. Typically, you begin with foreplay for approximately 15 minutes until you can tell that your wife is ready. The problem is, ready for what? Since, as with most women, she seldom orgasms during intercourse itself, should you continue stimulating her and bring her to a climax at this point?

Suppose you do bring her to orgasm. Now, the question is, how many times does she want to climax: once, twice, three times, more? Sure, you could ask her, but if you do, you're afraid she will feel rushed, as though you want to get it over so you can proceed with your own satisfaction. For her part, of course, she could just come right out and tell you that she wants to climax again, but she has learned to follow your lead. She doesn't want to impose on you. So, since you are the one in control, it's up to you to make your best guess as to which she would prefer and plow ahead.

If you do continue to stimulate her so that she can climax again, you are confronted with another uncertainty. How long should you wait after she has the first before stimulating her again so she can begin building toward her second? You know how sensitive you are after your own orgasm. You don't want to be touched at all for at least five minutes. It's actually painful. On the other hand, since she can climax again and again, women are obviously different.

Several times you started to ask her which she preferred, but you decided not to. After all, you didn't want to look like you had no idea what you were doing. Besides, if you started asking question after question, things could degenerate to the point where she would simply be issuing a series of orders, and you would lose the upper hand.

So you have decided to compromise. After her first orgasm you kiss her tenderly, wait a couple of minutes, and then begin again. But the fact that you still don't know for sure which would actually be better for her continues to bother you.

To complicate matters even further, the book you bought at the beginning of your marriage recommended that you vary your technique from time to time. So, reluctantly, you don't always bring her to climax first—though that would be much simpler. Instead, you have determined that every other time you make love you will initiate intercourse as soon as your wife becomes aroused from your foreplay.

Moving to the next step, of course, requires another decision: Which position should you use? In the early days of your marriage, you were uncertain about which of the book's recommended positions were best suited for the two of you. Several times, you almost lost the upper hand. To remove the guesswork, however, you quickly worked out a system which you continue to follow to this day.

You rely on three standard intercourse positions, using one of them, in turn, each time you make love. Variety without loss of control.

The next variable you face is length of intercourse. How long is it proper for you to continue before you allow yourself to climax? On one occasion, in the first year of your marriage, you noticed that your wife's lubrication began to diminish after about 15 minutes. Taking your cue from that incident, you settled on 12 minutes as the ideal length of intercourse to meet your wife's needs.

Sometimes, you have noticed, as you approach the 12-minute mark, your wife's movements seem to indicate that she would really like to continue. But you reluctantly conclude that it wouldn't be best for her at all. The friction could become quite painful for her. Better to be safe than sorry. So at the 12-minute mark you allow yourself to orgasm.

186

In some ways, this is the worst moment of all for you in lovemaking. The pleasure is intense for you, most certainly. That part you enjoy. But it is what you have to do to arrive at orgasm that disturbs you so deeply.

You have to surrender control.

It feels as though for the past 12 minutes you have been driving a race car on a narrow, winding mountain road. The car has been steadily accelerating, faster and faster. Suddenly, you see a sharp curve just ahead. Every instinct in your brain screams at you to slam on the brakes. But no, in order to experience orgasm, you have to stomp the gas pedal to the floor and take your hands off the wheel!

Orgasm occurs the moment you crash through the guardrail and plunge over the cliff into a free fall of 500 feet. The giddy, head-over-heels, heart-thumping feeling *is* exhilarating—that you can't deny. But even after this many years, it still scares you to death. All the way down you keep thinking, "I'm going to be smashed to pieces on the rocks!"

Consequently, as soon as you begin the plunge of your orgasm, you try to stay calm. As much as possible, you attempt to hold your feelings in check. You do your best to ride it out alertly as you fall, guarding against any untoward behavior. After all, it is common knowledge that when people's passions become aroused, they act less predictably. They might think they know themselves, but there is always the potential that the excitement will stir up something within them that no one has ever seen before.

On several occasions, this has very nearly happened to you. There have been times when your own pleasure blinded you for an instant and a wild thought or an unfamiliar desire suddenly inflamed your mind. As a result, you feel you have to monitor your lovemaking the same way a cook watches a pot to keep it from boiling over. When you start to get too carried away, you deliberately slow the pace, reach for your inner control know, and calmly turn down the flame.

After you have experienced your own muted orgasm, there is still the matter of your wife's to be dealt with, on those occasions when she has not climaxed prior to intercourse. The book you read had some very stern language for the inconsiderate man who rolls over and falls asleep after he is finished, failing to bring the same degree of pleasure to his wife. Consequently, for years it has been a point of pride with you to bring your wife to orgasm every time.

What truly puzzles you is that sometimes after intercourse your wife acts as though all she wants is for you to hold her. On several occasions when you began to caress her, she has actually told you, "Sweetheart, that's not necessary."

You are not about to be that selfish, however. After all, even with your mixed feelings toward orgasm, what would sex be without it?

Still, at such times it almost feels as though you are forcing your wife to climax. You can tell that she is struggling to cooperate, and that bugs you because you are doing it for her! It's a good thing you're in control. Otherwise, your wife might never experience the frequency of sexual release she requires.

Do you know what is so frightening about this hole of control you have dug for yourself? It is unlikely that anyone will ever be able to show you how much you and your wife are actually missing. Yours just isn't the kind of "problem" that shows up in the typical counseling room.

After all, the frequency with which you have sex probably falls within the average for your ages. You may not suffer from impotence or premature ejaculation. And what is your spouse going to complain about? Can you picture your wife asking to see her minister, her counselor, or her therapist, and whining, "In the past year, I've had to endure textbook-perfect sex!"

The typical marriage counselor is not going to say, "You poor thing! My heart goes out to you! Your husband is nothing but a heartless beast!" Instead, your counselor is much more likely to retort, "My advice to you is to grin and bear it, and to count your blessings!"

As a matter of fact, you can continue to make love as you are now doing for the rest of your lives without any apparent ill effect. Your dedication to absolute control assures you of a sex life that is superior to that of most couples. There is not a thing wrong with what you are doing... so long as you are content with above-average sex.

But in that case, what are you doing reading this book? If all you want is what you have, you've already read too far! The truth is, however, that you want more. You want it because you sense it is already there, just waiting for you and your spouse to reach out and experience. It's just that you're trying to figure out a way to grab it and still maintain total control!

Well, you can. Follow me carefully now: You do not have to lose control in order to have great sex. What you have to lose is your *fear* that you will lose control!

Were you able to identify with at least some of the thought patterns I described in the first part of this Doorway? I went into that much detail to enable you to gain the perspective that would help you see the truth. For the truth is, such a man is not in control. He is so full of fear that he is unable to allow either his wife or himself to experience everything they desire. And that is the opposite of what it means to be under true control.

Great sex requires great communication between two lovers. It is when you are too afraid to ask your wife what she wants that you are out of control. Knowledge is power—the power to thrill your wife and send her into orbit. Ignorance is weakness—the kind of weakness that simply doesn't have enough strength to maintain control.

The next time you fear you are about to lose control, ask yourself what it is you wish to control. Up to now about all you have been able to control is your level of conversation during sex. But your refusal to allow your wife to share her preferences has stripped you of a far more significant kind of control. Which would you rather steer: a model airplane or a Concord Jet?

You can fly the toy by yourself. All you have to do is read the instruction booklet. You don't have to ask anybody anything. Without question you will be in total control. But once again the question is, in control of what?

On the other hand, should you desire to soar in a Concord, reading a book or two just won't do. You are going to have to ask a lot of questions and follow a lot of instructions.

Before they will let you sit in the captain's seat of that awesome cockpit, you are going to have to demonstrate the ability to fly "blind," placing total trust in your instruments. And when it comes time to land that baby, you are going to have to maintain constant contact with the control tower, allowing them to talk you down.

Can you see the difference? The bigger the plane, the more vital is open communication *in order to maintain control.* But listening to your wife and responding sensitively to her every desire is only half the battle you must win if you desire true control. The other half is learning to implement a much more powerful degree of control . . . over yourself.

One of the secrets to great sex is the ability to give in to your passion. Your fear of doing so prevents you from exercising the level of self-control you actually desire! The key to excitability is vulnerability. Simply ask yourself, "Which requires greater personal control: to stand erect or to fall backward into someone's arms and trust that person to catch you?" The answer is obvious, isn't it? Even so, it requires much more "control" to let your passion go!

Do you know what you have been doing? You have been attempting to control the wrong thing! Trying to experience marvelous lovemaking by keeping the pot of your passion from boiling over is like trying to win the 100-meter dash by rapidly blinking your eyes. You're exercising the wrong set of muscles!

Make it your aim to control your fear, not your passion.

16

Let Go of Your Predictability

Your desire for sexual intensity does not mean that you should keep the pedal to the metal all the time. The more you let go of your inhibitions, the more you will want to hold on to your mystery, the more you will both come to value the element of surprise. Don't just flop back on the bed with the attitude, "Here it all is. What you see is what you get."

No, no, *Mon Cheri*. Keep him guessing. Whatever you do, don't let him think he has you all figured out. Just when he thinks he knows the next move you are going to make, change all the rules. In secure relationships there is a place, after all, for playing "hard to get."

Come up on her blind side. If you always begin your lovemaking by kissing her lips and gradually working your way down, it's time for a change. Next time start with her feet and work your way up!

Are you the verbal type? Then sometime (and be sure her mood is exactly right before you try this, or you could cook your goose good, Bud!) fix your blazing eyes on hers and, without ever unlocking your gaze and without saying a word, make love without kissing her once!

Or suppose you're the submissive one and your husband always takes the lead. Go out on a limb (literally) and become the aggressor for an evening. Mail him a letter that arrives at work (be sure his secretary doesn't read any letters marked "Personal"!) and give him explicit instructions for the night.

Tell him when and where you will meet him. Tell him what you want him to wear or not wear. Tell him what cologne you want him to have on, and where you want it applied.

When he arrives, give him no opportunity to take charge, as he usually does. Instead, start issuing "orders." Tell him what you as a woman need, which may be very different from his masculine perspective. Do not back off for a single moment—from beginning to end—until you have got precisely what you are after. It will give him something to think about while he's at his desk tomorrow.

Does that violate the scriptural principle of submission to your husband? Only if he protests! Certainly, if such an approach would make your husband uncomfortable, you should avoid it. But the truth is, your husband would most likely eagerly welcome such a surprise. If you doubt that, go ahead and ask him! If he says, "I'd love it!" then it qualifies as "submissive" behavior!

Don't forget that you can vary the setting in which you make love. Although by far the most comfortable and convenient, the bedroom is not the only cove available to you in your Garden of Eden. So long as you are confident of privacy, any room of the house is fair game... and presents its own challenge!

Think of the possibilities of that big recliner in the living room... the tub in the bathroom... the table in the kitchen... the couch in the den... the incline bench in the exercise room... the floor in front of the family room fireplace... the lawn tractor in the garage (motor running, of course)! Even the guest bedroom will provide a totally different feel for you in contrast to your own bed.

Nor are you limited to the confines of your own home. If you have a tall fence and short houses around you, take a sleeping bag into your backyard and enjoy the moon, the stars... and each other. Do not attempt this during mosquito season.

If you know of a private woods where you are absolutely certain you won't be disturbed, ask the owner's permission to take a walk and have a picnic. Seek out a hidden grove of trees, spread out your blanket, enjoy a simple lunch together... and a very elaborate dessert! A word to the wise: Since the nearest washbasin, tissues, and towels will be quite a distance away, be sure to pack your picnic basket with all the "comforts" of home.

"What about the backseat of our car?" you may ask, getting into the spirit of things. If you're game, why not? Just remember that those things don't have much room—nor do they provide much privacy. Don't pull off the road in an unknown spot where you might get bushwhacked by some flashlight-carrying mischief-makers. For that matter, you don't want some policeman tapping on your steamy window and asking to see your I.D.!

Don't allow the time of your lovemaking to slip into a rut, either! If you normally make love in the evening, why not set your alarm 30 minutes early and get your day off to a really great start? This is an especially good idea if you are one of those hard-driving couples who are ready for physical collapse when you hit the bed at night. Great lovemaking requires that you be able to summon from somewhere just a little bit of energy!

Some people skip lunch or eat light and go to the gym for a workout during the noon hour. You could meet each other back at the house and get your diet and exercise in a much more delightful way! If you don't live close enough to work to make that feasible, borrow a friend's nearby apartment. People who cheat on their spouses have been using that getaway method for a long time. Who better deserves such a break than the married couple dedicated to staying absolutely faithful?

Let go of the predictability of your attire, as well. If you always wear the same nightgown, the same pajamas, change them. Wear the bottom half only. Or the top half, with the bottoms missing. Or wear nothing. For total contrast, sometime make love with your street clothes on—shoes and everything!

Or slip into your husband's favorite shirt—wearing nothing else—and see if you can coax him away from his Monday Night Football game. Walk in innocently and stand by his chair, watching the game with him for a minute or two. Then, while you keep your eyes fixed on the television, take his hand and allow him to discover what you are—and are not—wearing! When he asks you just what you think you are doing, playfully tell him, "Shhhh! I'm really into this football game!"

If he loses interest in the Los Angeles Raiders and suddenly becomes more interested in making yardage with you, let him have you right there in his TV chair. While the athletes play their game, you can play yours. And keep his shirt on the whole time. He can push it up as far as he likes. Tell him to relax—it'll wash.

Or try this. Tell your wife to get totally undressed and to lie back on the bed and wait for you, eyes closed. Walk in and tell her to open her eyes—while you stand there decked out in your best suit or a rented tux! Make slow, tantalizing love to her, while remaining fully dressed. The contrast between her defenseless nudity and your formal attire will fire your imaginations and likely send you both off into some totally unexpected directions!

Be sure to browse through the lingerie department of a good store, or seek out a specialty shop that will spark your bedtime imagination. Sure, some of the stuff they sell is a little kinky, but your Aunt Matilda never has to know. Buy the most outlandish piece in the store with a smile, take a deep breath, and "kink" the night away!

Do you have a favorite cologne or after-shave? Be sure to change it every once in awhile. Do the same with your perfume. Go to the fragrance counter of a large department store and take a whiff of their top 25 bestsellers (you might want to take a couple of aspirin before you go to avoid a headache!). Select five fragrances that "do" something to you.

Stay with your standard fragrances most of the time, if you wish. An hour or two before you are going to make love, however, ask yourself what mood you wish to establish for the evening (or morning, or afternoon). If one of your new scents can help you establish that mood, splash (or dab) some on. Your lover will immediately notice the difference and wonder what you are up to, which is exactly the effect you want to establish. Keep 'em guessing!

If you are like many lovers, there is something romantic about spending the night together in a hotel room. But you don't have to wait for vacation to arrive or for a business trip. You don't even have to leave town—that just wastes precious time traveling that you could put to much better use!

Do this: Check in to a nearby hotel for the night. Dine together in the hotel restaurant or have a candlelight dinner in your room with the radio tuned to an easy-listening radio station. Make long, slow, leisurely love, then give in to the afterglow and drift off to sleep in each other's arms, even though it is still early. Sometime during the night, one of you will awaken. Your prior agreement is that the one who wakes up first starts the next lovemaking session... with a shower of gentle kisses and knowing caresses. What a wonderful way for your partner to be "aroused" from dreamland!

During the week you can get double use from the room. Next morning before you leave for work, don't turn in your key. Instead, ask for an extension of time before checkout. Then you can meet each other there for one more marvelous rendezvous during your lunch hour!

Do you have children? Try this: Rent the room on a Friday night and slip away after supper as soon as the baby-sitter arrives. For the next four or five hours, forget your parental responsibilities and become lovers only. Then return to reality and your home for the night.

Next morning after breakfast, take your kids to the hotel and let them enjoy the pool with you for a delightful time together as a family. Now that's having the best of both worlds!

If you already happen to be delighted with your love life just as it is, you may be reluctant to let go of your predictability. "After all," you may reason, "if it ain't broke, why fix it?"

Sometimes that is good advice. But in this case, it may not be. You may think things are really humming, but your spouse may have already reached the place where she knows the next five moves you are going to make and exactly how long you are going to take to make them, give or take ten seconds. She may be thinking to herself, "Let's see... he started nibbling my left earlobe at 8:30. That means I can get in another load of wash by 9:13, latest."

Six months later, by the time you notice her stifling a yawn and you begin to suspect that you just "may" have fallen into a rut, it will be too late. Your spontaneity will have been lost, and you will have dulled your lover's edge.

I'm not saying you cannot get it back. Of course you can. It's just that it is much harder to crank up something exciting when you are dead in the water than it is to go with the flow when you already have a running start!

So loosen up. Take some risks. Shake off your predictability.

"But what if the new stuff we try isn't as satisfying as our old standbys?"

What do you mean "if"? In most cases, I can promise you it won't be. When you try the floor instead of the bed, you may end up with carpet burns on your knees and a sore back the next morning! If you sneak out in the dead of night to enjoy your lover by the light of the silvery moon, you may both end up with the worst case of chiggers in three counties!

But that isn't the point. You were adventurers! You've made a special memory, even if it turned out to be a hilarious disaster! You stirred up the water of your marriage to keep it from going stagnant. You got each other's blood pumping again and put a little pink in each other's cheeks! Next day, the following week, five years from now, you'll still be able to chuckle over your little secret, shaking your heads at how crazy you both were to try some of the things you did.

When you return to your old favorites, you will appreciate them more. You will be reminded of why they work so well for you and why you eventually arrived at them the first time. By attempting the new, the different, even the zany, you will have actually extended the enjoyable life of the lovemaking methods you normally prefer!

But that's not all. Perhaps one time out of ten during your wild and woolly expeditions you will happen across something that makes you look at each other with big eyes and say, "Wow! I think we're going to have to try *this* one again!" Which means you will have just discovered a welcome addition to your growing repertoire of favorites.

Now for a word of balance. It is not necessary or even desirable to upset the entire applecart every time or every other time you make love. As we have just alluded to, there are probably some very good reasons why you have chosen your favorite positions, why you love to return to those special techniques that always work for you. Most lovers are loathe to give them up. So don't!

But vary your favorite techniques *each time* ever so slightly. If your wife is normally on her back when you begin your foreplay, turn her over on her tummy. If you catch yourself always starting out with a kiss on your husband's lips, this time begin with a kiss on his forehead. That one little adjustment will be enough to make him ask himself, "What's cooking?"... and to assure you that something will be.

17

Let Go of the Cares of the World

=====||=====

You cannot bring your latest problem with you into bed. Two's company; three's a crowd.

If you don't stop thinking about how poorly your daughter is doing in school, you are going to perform poorly after you enter the bedroom. If you just can't get out of your mind how disappointed you are in a friend who let you down, you are going to be a disappointment to your lover, whom you are also letting down.

Worries, distractions, anger, fears, hurts, problems, and hassles are death to great sex. No, you cannot avoid having them in your life. But it is essential that you learn to leave them at the bedroom door. If you don't, you are going to have one *more* problem to worry about: "Whatever happened to our sex life?"

Truly fulfilling lovemaking requires your full attention. But when you lay your head full of problems on your pillow, you are not all there for your spouse. Part of you is bent over the hood of your car, trying to figure out if you can coax another 10,000 miles out of its tired engine or whether you should trade vehicles within the next month. Part of you is hunched over the kitchen table shuffling through a stack of bills, wondering how you are going to make the mortgage payment this Friday because your health insurance company refused to pay $1,113.84 on your husband's knee surgery.

Those thoughts, you may have noticed, are not particularly sexy. And if your thoughts aren't sexy, it is exceedingly difficult for you to be.

It isn't very satisfying to your spouse to attempt to make love to someone who isn't all there. It makes him feel like an interruption. It makes him feel as though he isn't very important to you. When he realizes that you have your mind somewhere else, the desire he felt for you only moments before leeches out like the air from a rapidly deflating balloon.

You've got to stop it. In a thousand years, you wouldn't bring in a policeman to sit on the edge of your bed while you and your wife attempted to make love. So why do you insist on mentally bringing in the abrasive officer who wrote you a ticket for failing to come to a complete stop on your way home from work? That is an invasion of your privacy. He has no right to be in there with the two of you. Kick him out!

"But I can't help it!" you may insist. "I've tried. God knows I've tried. I do my best to push all my problems out of my mind, but it just doesn't work!"

There is no question that it is harder for some people to lay aside their problems than it is for others. It may be your personality to mull over every aspect of a situation nonstop until you have reached an acceptable solution. If that is who you are, a different approach is needed. It isn't enough to tell you to forget your problems for an hour. You would if you could, but you honestly don't know how. So let me show you in five not-easy-but-achievable steps.

1. Face the fact that you can't turn on until you learn to turn it off. Admit to yourself that you are undermining your own love life every time you fail to "dis-problem" at the same time you disrobe.

2. Before you enter the bedroom (or wherever you intend to make love this time!) make an appointment with your mate to discuss what is bothering you. Once you are assured that the problem is actually going to get the attention it deserves, you will find it much easier to let go of it for a short while. Of course, if the problem is with your spouse, you will want to rely on the strategy discussed in Secret Number One: "Do All Your Quarreling in One Hour a Week."

3. Understand your own needs. Because you are the conscientious type who is all over a problem like measles on a four-year-old, you can wear yourself to a frazzle. You need the love break much more than does your casual spouse! For your own health's sake, for the sake of your own emotional stability, you absolutely must tear free from your worries for a while. A totally absorbing romantic interlude is one of the few things powerful enough to pull you out of the daily quagmire, once you fully give in to it. It's a safety rope. Grab it!

4. The great news is that you *are* working on your problem when you let it go! It is a proven fact that one of the best things you can do to unravel a knotty problem is to walk away from it for a while. After you have wrestled with your difficulty for a period of time, it is possible to get so entangled that you have no chance whatever of pinning it to the mat. Your love break enables you to extricate yourself from the problem's clutches and come back to it a couple of hours later from another angle, rested, with fresh perspective.

5. You have no choice. Giving your mate your total attention during lovemaking is not an option. It is not merely something that would be nice to try every once in a while. It is an absolute necessity. You rob your lover and you cheat yourself when you fail to give absolutely everything you've got.

You are too nice to let that continue to happen. You care too deeply about your lover's happiness to allow your mate to pay that kind of price. Therefore, you will hand your problems to Jesus to oversee while you and your mate take time out to do what lovers do.

Do you know what you are going to find? From time to time you are going to find that some of your difficulties will have actually improved while you were busy with more "pressing" matters! After that happens to you on several occasions, who knows? Turning to Jesus in matters like these might become a whole new way of life.

18

Let Go of False Propriety

===||===

P ropriety" is a good word, in its place. Most of the time we use the word "propriety" to describe behavior that is socially acceptable in public. Certainly, the two of you must be appropriate when you are around other people, no matter how much you love each other and no matter how much you long to express that love. Consideration for the sometimes delicate feelings of others demands a constant awareness of what is fitting and proper.

Some people battle with the concept of propriety much more than others. If you can rip out a loud belch in public without giving it another thought, you probably don't have to worry about crippling propriety in the bedroom! In fact, you might want to pick up an etiquette book and brush up on your manners, just to be on the safe side.

On the other hand, you may be the type who would rather choke to death on a sneeze rather than allow the tiniest hiss of luncheon air to escape the flare of your left nostril. If that is who you are, accept it as a warning signal. It is quite likely that you are going to have trouble freeing yourself from an overwhelming sense of false propriety when you are all alone with your spouse.

Lest you misunderstand, we are not talking about becoming rude, lewd, or crude. We are talking about the freedom to breathe. We are talking about the joy of letting down your hair and being everything God made you to be. We are talking about deliverance from the uncomfortable sense that you are violating someone else's arbitrarily devised code of action or set of rules.

Everyone needs to step offstage periodically. Everybody needs frequent breaks from the cameras and hot lights. For your health's sake, you have to take yourself off display, turn off the microphones, shut down the tape recorders, and just be you. Otherwise, the stress of having to be "on" without respite will exact a vicious price on your body and on your emotional well-being.

Time alone to yourself can help to fulfill this need, but only partially. What you really need is several good friends. One definition of a true friend is someone with whom you can cast off the maddening restraints of polite society. Since some of those restraints involve clothing and sexual behavior, however, your spouse is the only person with whom you can be true "friends" all the way!

If you are a woman who has a strong sense of propriety, sex may provide you with your ultimate challenge. Because you are deeply in love with your husband, you have learned how to make yourself function sexually. But your deep, dark secret may be that you dread it before it happens, endure it while it is happening, and loathe yourself after it has happened.

In fact, there are only two positive emotions that you may be able to associate with having sex. The first is a sense of accomplishment that you were able to provide your husband with something that he obviously needs. The second is an overwhelming sense of relief that the ordeal is finally over.

Yes, sometimes you experience pleasure during sex, but the moment you do, you are stabbed with a sharp sense of guilt. "I can't believe that felt good!" you castigate yourself. "What kind of person must I be to actually enjoy doing something like this? I dare not give in to this feeling. If I do, there's no telling what kind of person I'll become!"

So you refuse to surrender to your own body's desires, keeping your natural sexual responsiveness under tight control. The prospect of engaging in totally uninhibited sex with your spouse seems inconceivable.

If this is who you are, as you have read these pages, you have become increasingly distraught. It is extremely unlikely, in fact, that you are the one who purchased this book. In all probability, it was your husband who bought the book, and whose excited insistence that it would be great if you read it together is the only reason you now hold it in your hands. That... and your guilt. Although your husband senses your sexual reticence, you probably haven't opened up and told him exactly how you feel. You don't want him to think less of you, and you certainly don't want him to experience rejection. You love your husband with all your heart—you really do! And that is why, for all these years, you have struggled internally.

You know why your husband has bought this book and why he wants so badly for you to read it. He thinks that all you need to do is read a few pages, loosen up a little, and everything will be fine. He has absolutely no concept of the seriousness of your sexual blockage.

Your husband is aware, of course, that you seldom if ever initiate lovemaking, but he probably attributes it to his belief that you are merely shy. Your reticence may have driven him to the bookstore many times, thinking that all he needed to do was improve his technique to turn you into the woman of his dreams. But the more of those "experts'" suggestions he has tried with you, the longer he has extended his foreplay, the farther you have retreated into your shell.

You seldom if ever orgasm, but you have faked it many times. When your husband whispers afterward, "Was it good for you, too, Sweetheart?" you have tried to assure him that it was, with all the false enthusiasm you were able to muster.

It's almost like being at a dinner party you are socially obligated to attend, isn't it? You have absolutely no desire to be there, but you have no choice. So you make the best of it. No matter how boorish the conversation, you smile and nod, and sometimes you even fake a laugh when you can tell your dinner companion has reached his awful story's punch line.

Propriety.

You're in prison, aren't you? You feel trapped, stifled, controlled by the expectations of others. But there is nothing you can do about it, you tell yourself, because after all, these are the rules of society. One must go to dinner parties when invited. It would be impolite to refuse. One must participate when one's husband desires sex. Everyone knows it is part of the obligation of marriage.

Propriety.

I cannot in these few pages even begin to address the full scope of your burden. You need at least several months of highly skilled, tender, sensitive, professional counseling. But because such people may be hard to find where you live, let me at least point you in the right direction.

First of all, please understand that you probably have a genetic predisposition for your highly developed sense of doing what is proper. All you have to do is investigate your family tree, and chances are excellent that you will discover one or more relatives who have passed on to you the characteristics with which you now struggle.

But the good news is this: You are who you are for a wonderful reason: God made you this way! And He is very pleased with His work. You are beautifully made and marvelously fashioned. Before we go any further, allow yourself the luxury of basking in that thought until you can sincerely thank God that you are you.

Do you still need to change your attitude toward lovemaking? Yes. But you will never succeed by fighting your basic personality. That's like asking an eagle to gallop or a racehorse to fly. Both are beautiful, impressive, and fast, but each has its own way of getting where it needs to go.

For purposes of illustration, let's call you an eagle. There is a reason that to this very day you have struggled unsuccessfully to enjoy lovemaking: You have been attempting to get there by using your legs! But as an eagle, your legs are not your strength. As long as you attempt to "run" toward your goal, you will continue to be trampled in the dust.

It's time to use your wings.

I'm going to recommend that you remain a person of high propriety. In fact, I am going to suggest that your lovemaking difficulties have arisen because, up to now, your propriety standards have not been high enough! Allow me to explain.

Suppose you had been invited to a formal dinner in Washington, D.C., for which you had purchased a new pair of shoes. By the time you arrived, you had discovered that they were too narrow in the toe. Your feet were killing you! Question: Upon arrival, would you take your shoes off at the door and give your astonished hosts a helpless shrug as you spent the rest of the evening in your stocking feet? Of course not. The very idea nearly brings on an attack of angina!

So far, so good. Now suppose you have been invited to a formal dinner at a traditional home in Japan. Upon entering the house, you notice 15 or 20 pairs of shoes neatly lined in a row just inside the door. Another couple entering with you at the same time begins removing their shoes, as the others have done. Question: Will you, for the sake of propriety, staunchly refuse to do likewise, and proudly insist on keeping your shoes on your feet throughout the remainder of the evening? Of course not. Once again, the very idea nearly brings on an attack of angina!

But wait a minute. Explain to me how it is that in one place you would refuse to remove your shoes, but in the next place you would refuse to leave them on.

"That should be totally obvious," I can imagine you would reply. "At a formal gathering in Washington, propriety demands that one keep one's shoes on at all times. In Japan, however, the rules are reversed. In that country, propriety demands that one remove one's shoes upon entering a traditional home."

Please hear what you just said: *When you change locations, propriety demands that you change behavior.* In fact, wouldn't you agree that to behave identically in both places would be the height of *impropriety*?

"That is correct."

Do you know what you are doing every time you enter the bedroom with your husband? You are forgetting that propriety demands a change of behavior with a change of place! In effect, you are attempting to run the 440 in your high heels. You are trying to take a bubble bath while wearing an expensive evening gown!

No, lovemaking is not acceptable at a dinner party, and that is why you keep having so much trouble in the bedroom. You keep trying to apply the behavioral rules you learned for a dinner party! And that is a clear case of misapplication. Do you know why you are doing that? Probably because nobody ever got around to teaching you the rules of propriety for lovemaking!

That's what every one of the Doorways in this Secret is all about: lovemaking propriety. So feel free to read, to absorb, and to learn. There is a world of hope for you! If you have the capacity to change your behavior when you enter Japan, that proves you are flexible. In that country, you shed your shoes. In lovemaking, you shed your inhibitions.

To do any less would be the height of impropriety.

Let Go of Your Preoccupation with Sex

19

W hat an unexpected way to end our "Let Go" series of Doorways! We've devoted this entire Secret thus far to helping you open up and see your range of godly loving options as unlimited. Are we now reversing our position and throwing cold water on the entire process by suggesting lovemaking without sex? What an anticlimax!

But stay with us now. This Doorway is no backward step. Rather, it will open up for you an exciting, entirely new dimension.

Each of us has a profound need for physical affirmation. We love to be caressed, stroked, fondled, kissed, tickled, licked, hugged, squeezed, scratched, held, nuzzled, brushed, massaged, handled, felt, explored, rubbed, smoothed, touched. Sexual loving meets part of that need—a very vital part. But the touching that leads to or accompanies sex cannot begin to meet the whole of our need for physical affirmation. Nonsexual touching is magic. It says to the recipient, "You're here. You exist. You matter to me. You're important. I cannot merely intellectualize your value to me. I must use my hands, my lips, my fingernails, my teeth, my eyelashes, my hair, my entire physical being to find release and expression for the uncontainable love uncontrollably welling up inside me for you, you, you!"

When you walk past your wife in the kitchen without touching her, you may unwittingly convey a subliminal message that says, "I don't have time to acknowledge your existence now. Something else is more important to me than you are. Besides, we aren't going to have sex right before dinner, so what would be the point?" Never mind that your male mind rejects the preposterous irrationality of that thought. You would be shocked at how many wives wrestle with something akin to those very emotions, either consciously or subconsciously. A "Hi, Honey. How was your day?" isn't enough. Words are important, but they can be tossed off too quickly, too cheaply, too thoughtlessly. Your wife needs to know that she can make the world stop for you. Your darling needs visible, tangible, physical proof that her mere presence is enough to rip your attention away from every other competing interest in your life.

When you walk in the door, hang up your coat, glance over the newspaper headlines, scratch the dog behind the ears, return a couple of stray toys to their shelf, loosen your tie, then come across your wife in the living room and give her a hug, you've done well. But even better, when you walk in the door, make a beeline to wherever she is, drop your briefcase in the middle of the floor, and swallow her up in a long embrace interspersed with kisses, nuzzles, and "Oh Baby, I've missed you!"

In the first instance, you have told her that she fits somewhere in your world. But in the second, you have communicated to her loudly and clearly that she *is* your world! If you really need to, ask her which message she prefers to receive.

If you could come up with a thousand ways a day to convey to your wife, "More than what I want *from* you, I just want *you!*" it would never be too much. Your words launch the message...but your touch brings it home. A woman needs, desires, longs for, and craves her mate's acknowledgment of her intrinsic value.

And so does a man. Many husbands spend their entire lives in a futile attempt to experience through their careers what only their wives can convey with the awesome power of their feminine touch. As mysterious as it may sound, eight hours of a man's accumulated workplace frustration can be soothed away by 15 minutes of his head in his wife's lap, her fingers lightly tracing his facial features and running back and forth through his hair.

Is there anything sexual about such caresses? No. Is it, perhaps, early foreplay? No. Rather, it is physical, emotional, mental, and somehow inexplicably even spiritual healing conveyed solely through loving, nonerotic touch. I cannot explain it to you. Words are totally inadequate in this realm. But I can testify that Judy and I have personally found it to be true.

This then is the mystical, deeply satisfying dimension of nonsexual lovemaking. It does not end in orgasm...but in restoration. It does not climax in a spasm of blinding light...but melts into a soul-satisfying sense of utter wholeness and tender union.

As you constantly, consistently minister to one another through life-giving touch, you will provide the vital, loving context out of which your sexuality will achieve its greatest meaning and find its fullest expression.

Don't Be Afraid of Old-Fashioned Romance!

20

Having absorbed all of the outlandish things before and after this Doorway, please don't let go of old-fashioned romance. A thousand books have alluded to soft music and dinner by candlelight, but unoriginal though it may sound, it still works—again, and again, and again!

Take moonlit walks together—not briskly, arms pumping for exercise, but strolling hand-in-hand, sharing your thoughts, stopping every little bit to embrace or to plant an affectionate kiss on your lover's cheek.

Set aside unhurried time to bathe each other—lovingly, tenderly washing your spouse's body with a soapy cloth and allowing your mate to do the same for you. Sure, sometimes it will lead to more, either in the tub or after you have briskly toweled each other off. But there will be other times that you will lazily move from the bath to the bed and fall contentedly asleep in one another's arms. It doesn't always have to end in intercourse to qualify as romance!

Sometime surprise your spouse for a special occasion by secretly making all the arrangements for an overnight trip. One year for Valentine's Day my wife and I got into the car together after an evening church service. Our children rode with another couple, whom my wife assumed we were going to meet for pizza at a local restaurant. Little did she know that I had something altogether different in mind!

When I turned onto the highway, Judy asked me what I was doing. And that's when I announced that I had booked an out-of-town honeymoon suite for the next two nights, with a day of snow skiing sandwiched in between! The fact that she nearly froze to death waiting for me underneath a snow-blowing machine, and that I came close to killing myself on one of the expert slopes is beside the point. It was romantic. We made a memory, and we laugh about it to this day.

Maybe one of your wife's fantasies is to make love in a barn. She should have to say no more! Pick the right time of year when the straw is fresh and sweet-smelling, locate just the right barn, obtain permission from the farmer, explaining that you would like to rent his barn for a two-hour "meeting" (that's the truth!), and you're all set. Dressed in outdoor garb, secure the door behind you and escort your country lass up to the hay loft where the two of you can enjoy a good, old-fashioned, time-honored "roll in the hay"!

Do you own one of those detachable shower massage units? If not, you may want to buy an inexpensive one. It will be far cheaper than dinner at a good restaurant. Invite your husband to step into the shower with you some morning and take turns giving each other lots of attention in a creative, invigorating, watery cascade!

Or pick up some baby oil and take turns giving each other a 30-minute, full-body massage. Whether or not it leads to a full-blown lovemaking session is beside the point. You'll have made each other feel utterly relaxed and absolutely marvelous!

This old-time standby still has charm, as well: Rent or borrow a rowboat and go for a slow-motion boat ride on a silvery lake. Try it late enough in the evening to avoid the afternoon heat, and early enough so that you can watch the sun go down in the west, just as you finish your private lovers' excursion. Unless the lake is private and your are both excellent swimmers, I recommend that you wait to follow up on any overly amorous inclinations, however, until you are safely ashore!

Making love in front of the fireplace has been a centuries-old favorite, but why not take a cue from one man I know who made their fireplace the centerpiece of a surprise present for his wife? It was the Friday night before her Saturday birthday, and she had no idea that anything unusual was up. As soon as she entered the bathroom to take her usual shower, her husband Bill leapt into action.

He moved the mattress he had made up earlier into the family room in front of a crackling fire he had built in the fireplace. A multitude of candles were lit and placed around the room. He arranged a dish of gourmet candies beside the mattress and positioned two roses on their pillows for symbolic effect. The family room was now transformed into the scene of an about-to-be garden of marital delights.

Rushing back to the bathroom door, Bill waited for his unsuspecting wife to finish her shower. As she opened the door, Bill took her hand and led her into the family room, whereupon she saw his elaborate preparations and began to giggle.

True lover that he is, Bill opened up with an hour-long nonsexual massage, during which he fed her the candies, one by one. He threw in a few other niceties for good measure.

Later on, Bill admits, things did get very interesting on the mattress in front of the fireplace. Based upon his wife's response, Bill is convinced that this one will go down as one of his wife's favorite birthday presents ever. Hearing him talk, you can't help but conclude that it wasn't exactly a boring experience for him either!

A picnic in the park, lunch hour at the museum, roller-skating at the rink, bowling at the alley, a concert at the stadium, shooting billiards in the parlor, tennis at the club—all of these can be old-fashioned dates, romantic times that get you laughing, focused on one another, and doing the same thing at the same time, connecting on the same wavelength. These and a hundred other common, easily available activities can be the backdrops for times of special warmth, closeness, and, if it happens, eventual intimacy.

In your all-out desire to circle the moon and touch the stars, don't leave out the more obvious paths of romance that have stood the test of time. Everything God has created is good.

Savor it all.

Why Not Put Some "Tsachaq-ing" Behavior in Your Love Life?

21

Sometimes when you come together in passionate love-making, you make classical music. The string section soars, the timpani boom, and the cymbals crash. But sexual loving doesn't always have to be so deadly serious. There are plenty of times when your lovemaking can assume the tone of a playful ragtime session, complete with upright piano, oom-pa tuba, and a set of click-clackety musical spoons!

When you've had to deal with problem after problem all day long, you need a break. That's why some husbands hear their wiped-out wives plead, "Not tonight, Dear."

But it's not really lovemaking that is being rejected, it's stress. So lighten up! When the tension is thick and the energy level is low, don't be afraid to walk into the bedroom with a playful gleam in your eye and declare, "Attention! For the next 90 minutes absolutely nothing serious will be allowed to take place!"

For that matter, don't wait for a disastrous day to give yourself permission to exercise your sexual sense of humor. Sex games can be exactly what your tightly wound emotions need to relieve the stress of everyday living.

"Hold it!" I can just imagine you saying. "I'm ready—and more than willing—to enjoy everything God blesses, but before I read any further, I would love to have just one scriptural hint that sex "play" is within God's ideal for our marriage. I'm not saying it's essential, but it would certainly be nice!"

Sure. I understand. Let's go to Genesis, the "book of beginnings" for just that "hint" of biblical sex play you requested.

In order to escape the famine in Beer Lahai Roi, Isaac moved for a time to Gerar. There, he repeated the deception of his father, Abraham, before him and told everyone who inquired about his wife, Rebekah, that she was his sister. He did this because Rebekah was so beautiful that he was afraid the men of Gerar would kill him to get her.

For a long time the ruse worked. Then one day, Abimelech king of the Philistines, looked down from his window and saw Isaac and Rebekah behaving in a most unseemly way for two people who were supposed to be brother and sister!

Afterward, Abimelech called for Isaac and rebuked him for hiding the fact that Rebekah was really his wife.

The question is, what were Isaac and Rebekah doing? God gave Moses the Hebrew word *Tsachaq* to describe the activity in which they were engaged. The more staid New International and New American Standard versions of the Bible translate it "caressing." The Revised Standard Version tries "fondling," and the Living Bible opts for "petting."

Leave it to the King James Version of 1611, however, to provide us with the most literal rendering! For hundreds of years, Christians cocked an eyebrow when they read:

> And it came to pass, when he had been
> there a long time, that Abimelech king of the

Philistines looked out at a window, and saw,
and, behold, Isaac was *sporting* with Rebekah
his wife.[1]

"Sporting!" Does the Hebrew really support "sport"?
It sure does. *Tsachaq* is frequently translated elsewhere
as "entertainment," "jesting," "laughing," "making sport,"
"mocking," and "playing"! In fact, *Tsachaq* comes from the
Hebrew root "to laugh!"

Did God select *Tsachaq* because it was the only Hebrew
word that described sexual behavior between husband and
wife? Far from it! He could have chosen the much milder
ohab, which can be translated "caresses," or *chabaq*, which
means "embracing."

For that matter, God could have told Moses, "Let's use
the word *shakab*, which can be translated "sexual rela-
tions."

Shekabah ("intercourse") and *shekobeth* ("copulation")
were also available to Him. In fact, let's face it: God could
have remained entirely circumspect and simply stayed
with *naga*, which means "touching."

But He didn't. With all those choices available to Him,
God insisted on using the very word that every Jew associated with entertainment, laughing, and playing. Why?
Because they were, in fact, engaged in shocking *Tsachaq-
ing!*

Look. If in Holy Scripture God was not ashamed of
playful sexual behavior, why should we be? Our position is,
if it was good enough for Isaac and Rebekah, it's good
enough for us!

The next three Doorways feature a total of 11 *Tsachaq-
ing!* (pronounced "shocking!") games you can play that are
guaranteed to get you laughing and loving—or at the very
least to start your own creative juices flowing. Once we get

you started, you'll be able to invent as many *Tsachaq*-ing! games as you like.

(Warning: If there is in your personality even the slightest possibility that you could be offended by a no-holds-barred approach to love play, please skip the next three Doorways. What comes next is meant only for the most playful, liberated lovers among us!)

Old Favorites ...
With a New Twist!

H ow many parlor/backyard games do you know how to play? As you will see from the next three examples, all you have to add is a little ingenuity and each of them can be transformed into a lover's delight!

High Stakes Cards

Select a fairly short card game for two players. Play begins when each of you writes down on a slip of paper an intimate "favor" that you would love to receive from the other. Turn your paper over and do not reveal what you have written.

Now that you are properly motivated, proceed with the game as usual. Play with all your might, because whichever of you wins gets to claim your chosen prize!

If, for example, you win, and your piece of paper says that you would love to be kissed over every inch of your body for five solid minutes, your spouse has to pay up, right on the spot!

It's a Whole New Game!

This one works with any board game which requires

that activity cards be frequently drawn during the course of the game. But here's the catch: Before the game begins, substitute your own cards for the ones that came with the game!

Give your spouse a dozen or so blank cards to fill out, and take the same number for yourself. Make half of them sensual rewards and the other half sexy "penalties." When finished, keep what you have written a secret, shuffle both sets of cards together, turn them face down, and start the game.

When the game calls for you to draw a card, you are required to perform whatever the card commands. But be careful what you write. You might end up having to obey your own "penalty" card!

Charade Parade

When it is your turn, select a sexual treat that you are both sure to enjoy but have never shared—or at least haven't indulged in for a while. You have 60 seconds to silently convey what it is to your mate, being sure to adhere to all the usual rules for the game of Charades.

Oh, yes—there is one additional restriction. You cannot point to the body part(s) involved in the sexual treat you are attempting to portray!

If your spouse guesses correctly within the time limit, you immediately get to enjoy the activity you just described. You both win! If, however, time expires before your spouse guesses correctly, you must reveal the treat, which is now forbidden to you for the rest of the day. You both lose! Ah, but don't lose heart. Next, it is your spouse's turn. Sooner or later, somebody is bound to guess something!

There is an interesting delayed reaction to Charade

Parade. For the next week or so, you will both find yourselves mysteriously eager to sample the delights that were forbidden to you on game day because you failed to guess them in time!

To Share If You Dare!

ost lovemaking games are physical. These four are especially so. Just as with the rest, they are not for everybody. But if from them you glean even one idea that puts a sparkle in your eye and an unforgettable night on your calendar, then they will have served their purpose.

Just a word of caution: If the previous Doorway was a little too much for you, then we hereby hang out the "Do Not Enter" sign over this one!

Blind Man's Bluff

Only no one's bluffing! Ask your husband's permission to blindfold him during your next lovemaking session. If he wants to know why, tell him the only way he will find out is to cooperate!

If he agrees, your task is simple: Remove all his clothes and take total advantage of him in his defenseless state. Lead him around the room from chair, to stool, to bed. If you are alone in the house, take him from room to room to disorient him. Bend him over and stretch him out on unpredictable surfaces.

Repeatedly surprise him. Touch him wherever and however you wish. And guide his hands, fingers, mouth, and tongue where they will do you the most good. He'll love it...and so will you! The more of a "take charge" type he is, the more it will do you both a world of good.

Compliments 'N Kisses!

Draw up two chairs facing each other, pads and pencils in hand. Number your papers from one to ten. Together agree upon ten body features (eyes, hair, breasts, etc.) and list them beside each number.

Your husband goes first, paying as many different compliments to you concerning your first feature on his list as he can come up with in the space of one minute. You announce when his time is up and write down beside item number one how many compliments he paid your eyes, for example. Now it's your turn to see how many compliments you can pay his eyes! Here are the rules:

1. The compliments must be accurate.
2. The compliments must be sincerely delivered.
3. The compliments must be paid while looking into the recipient's eyes.

As you can easily see, the person who goes second has the advantage since he or she has just heard all the compliments paid to that same body feature by the other spouse! Therefore, after you have gone second on the first feature, you must now go first on your spouse's second body feature—complimenting his lips, for example. After you have finished, he will then compliment your lips, and you will once again record each other's scores. On the third feature—your breasts, for example—it is again your husband's turn to go first, and so on.

When you have complimented all ten of each other's features, it's time to tally up the final score. Highest total number wins. If you are the winner, your husband must give you as many kisses as you paid him compliments... on the appropriate spot!

For example, if you paid him six compliments for his big brown eyes, then he will plant six loving kisses on your gently closed eyes, three for your right, and three for your left. If he goes too fast, tell him to take his time and kiss you with feeling so you can enjoy your reward for being so complimentary! If your husband wins, of course, it is you who must pucker up!

Another variation of this game allows you to declare a winner after each body feature is mentioned. You might win the "eyes," but your husband could very well win the "lips." The rewards are dispensed immediately, before going on to the next feature!

If you have less time, you can play the game listing only five body features, three, or even one. What a great way to pass the time while you are driving somewhere in the car, or while you are standing in one of those long lines at an amusement park during vacation! In those cases you will, of course, have to save the "payoff" until later!

A less sexual but deeply rewarding variation is to select personal characteristics to compliment rather than body features. If you have time for three, you might agree on honesty, sense of humor, and love for God. Since it is kind of tough to be kissed on your "sense of humor," if you are the winner, you get to designate exactly where you want to receive any—or all—of the kisses you have coming!

Not only is this a fun game to play, with lots of laughter and lovely "smooches" at the end, but it does wonders for your relationship. First, it feels great to hear all of those compliments during the game. But the best part is that the more you play it, the more you get into the habit of saying lots of nice things to one another. Better still, you can't say them until you think them, which sparks genuine admiration and thanksgiving in each of your hearts for your spouse!

Wanna Bet?

How do you settle differences of opinion in your household? This game is a simple takeoff on the familiar friendly wager. But not only is it much more fiscally responsible, it can add a definite spark to an otherwise ho-hum day!

When was the last time you were in a hurry for a dinner engagement or other appointment, and your spouse said, "Weren't you supposed to have turned left on Elm Street?" and you replied, "No, no, you've got it confused with Oak Street. We don't turn until we've gone another six blocks further."

If your spouse is the kind who automatically backs down and says, "Oh. You're probably right," this game is not going to work for you. But if your spouse is the kind who retorts, "No, I think you are the one who is confused. I'm sure it's Elm Street where you should have turned," then this game is a sure winner for the two of you!

When your spouse takes a firm position on a minor issue that is opposite from your own, all you have to do is reply, "Wanna bet?"

The fun ingredient here is that you are not betting money but sexual favors! Most lovers have their favorite delights that they can never get enough of. What an opportunity to turn an ordinary automobile ride into a scintillating opportunity!

When you ask your spouse, "Wanna bet?" your spouse asks, "What are the stakes?"

You may reply, "If we're supposed to turn on Oak Street, you have to make love to me tonight, using five different positions before you climax!"

And your spouse may reply, "Fine—but if we should have turned on Elm, you have to use nothing more than your mouth."

If the stakes are agreeable, you then answer, "Done!"

If either of you is unwilling to accept the stakes, you can dicker back and forth until you reach something equitable—or one of you will be forced to back down!

A simple reminder: If you are the "loser," be sure you pay up enthusiastically and promptly. After all, you may win the next wager, and you want to be sure you have set a first-class example for your spouse to follow!

Guess What?

To prepare for this game, each of you must collect ten different office, household, sports, or food items. Put them in separate bags and secure the tops so neither of you has any idea what items the other has selected.

Next, inform each other of the prize you would like to receive, if you should be the winner. Now that you know what you are playing for, flip a coin to see who goes first. If you win the toss, you get to blindfold your husband and lead him to the bed, asking him to lie on his back.

Next, remove all his clothes. Reach into your sack and pull out the first item, placing it anywhere on his body that you like. He has ten seconds to guess what it is. Keep track of his hits and misses as you proceed through all the items in your sack.

Next, it's his turn to blindfold you and lead you to the bed. You have a slight advantage because you know what score you have to beat! Highest number guessed right wins the agreed-upon prize.

Oh yes. For the really daring couple, there is another version of this game, as well. No, we are not going to provide the details. Just think about it. If the "other" version is really "right" for you, we won't have to say another word!

Mind Games

As well-read lovers, you may have heard some variation of this one: "What's your most important sex organ? Wrong! It's your mind!"

And so it is. Without the active involvement of our imaginative minds, human sexual activity would quickly degenerate to an animalistic level. We would experience far less pleasure, which means that few of us would have sex nearly so often.

If you have never thought much about it, you should. As lovers, you already have active sexual imaginations. But once you recognize the vital role your mind plays in the intensity and total satisfaction of your sex life, you can begin to unleash its awesome power on purpose.

Let me give you a simple example. Suppose your wife walks up to you and looks deeply into your eyes. Never lowering her gaze, she wordlessly unbuttons your shirt and spreads it wide, exposing your naked chest. Next, with a sly smile she extends her middle finger and, lightly touching her fingernail to your chin, slowly draws a straight line along your neck, between your nipples, over your belly, and all the way down to your belt buckle.

Question: During the two minutes it takes her to complete that little exercise, what has been happening to every cell in your body? Right.

But why?

Only your mind, my friend, only your mind. Apart from the significance your two busy little brains attached to her fingernail trail, there was nothing inherently sexy about it. If the two of you had not "made something out of nothing," the only urge you would have had when she was finished would have been to shiver, scratch the place she had tickled, and with some irritation quickly rebutton your shirt.

What a magnificent, glorious, unspannable gap there is between man and animal!

Let the four games in this final Doorway remind you to breathe a prayer of thanks to your Creator for giving you such an awesome mind.

The Commercial

For this one, you'll need either an audio- or a videotape recorder/player. You'll also need to be a real "ham" to pull it off!

Start listening to the radio and watching television, on the lookout for commercials that have double entendre possibilities: "We do it all for you!" "It's the real thing!" "Have it your way!" "When it absolutely, positively, has to be there overnight." "So squeezably soft!" "Just do it." The list of possibilities is virtually endless.

Once you have decided on your favorite, wait until your spouse is not around. Then, building on the theme you have chosen, tape a 60-second "commercial," focusing on one of the more "interesting" parts of your anatomy as the "product" you are trying to sell!

Once you have your "commercial" in the can, bide your time until the moment is right. Some evening when you are "in the mood" but your husband is only sleepy, turn out the lights and slip under the covers as though you had no intention of doing anything but falling asleep. Then, in the darkness, announce brightly, "We'll return to 'Sweet Dreams' in just a moment. But first, a word from our sponsor!" Then reach over to the nightstand and punch the "start" button on your cassette tape player ... or, if you have a television and VCR in your bedroom, hit the remote!

After your "commercial" is over, and if you have done your job well, chances are your formerly sleepy hubby will be ready to "purchase" the "product" you have just "advertised," right on the spot! You can tease him by replying, "One moment, please. I'll have to check and see if we still have that 'item' in stock!"

A word to the wise: Keep your "commercials" under lock and key at all times!

Math Concentration

Each of you writes out an addition problem for the other. To make the contest fair, your problems will have to be the same length—say, eight columns of three-digit numbers. Your wife goes first, and you time how long it takes her to arrive at the answer. When she finishes, it's your turn and she times you.

From there, you progress to one 20-digit subtraction problem each, and on through multiplication and division. After each of you has worked all four simple but lengthy problems, you grade each other's papers. Whichever of you gets the most answers right wins. In the case of a tie, the shortest time prevails. Simple, huh?

By the way, did I remember to mention that before you start you both have to take off all your clothes and that you each have to work your problem standing up? Hmmm. Seems like there was something else, too.

Oh yes. While your wife works her problem, you're allowed to kiss her, tickle her, caress her, and stroke her wherever and however you wish—you know, just to see if it might possibly distract her a wee bit from the task at hand. Of course, when it becomes your turn, she gets to do the same to you!

The winner gets to name the "method" he or she chooses to relieve all that built-up "mathematical" tension!

Cellular Code

Perhaps you read the story about the politician who used his cellular phone to set up a hotel tryst with a woman. Not until local radio and television stations began to play excerpts of the conversation did he realize that cellular transmissions can be eavesdropped on and recorded!

As lovers, you have the right to say whatever you want to say to each other, whenever you want to say it. But you also have a right to your privacy! Even if you don't carry a cellular phone in your car, there is always the possibility that someone will listen in or overhear a telephone conversation between you and your lover. For that matter, what about those times when your wife calls you at work and there are several other people with you in the room?

Wouldn't it be nice if you could speak as intimately with each other as you wished, without getting yourselves teased unmercifully for months afterward? Well, you can. And it's fun, too! Here's how.

Some weekend afternoon before you make love, take the time to assign innocent names to all of each other's "crucial" body parts. You get to invent the names for your husband's, and he has the privilege of naming yours.

As he lies back in bed against his pillow, fondly look him over and give each part a kiss as you name it: "I dub thee Larry... I dub thee Norman and thee Nicholas... I dub thee Sir William the Great... I dub thee Bob, and thee Barney... I dub thee Charlie, and thee Chauncy... and lastly, I dub thee Arnold!"

Then, it's your turn to arrange yourself just so and allow your husband to enjoy a long, loving look. Let him plant an affectionate kiss on each of your feminine charms as he names them: "I title thee Louella... I title thee Tammy and thee Tania... I title thee Claretta, and thee Pamela, and thee Lady Katherine... I name thee Babs, and thee Brenda... and lastly, I name thee Shelley!"

That's all there is to it. From that point on, it's nothing but fun: "Hi, Sweetheart, how has your day been? Say, have you been in touch with Claretta today? No? Well, you really should try to get in contact with her before tonight, if at all possible.... Yes, it's urgent."

Or, "How are Bill and Kathy doing? Do you think you could ask him to stop by and spend a little time with her? I think it would do them both a world of good!"

Even answering machines can be put to good use: "Yes, I'm calling to leave a message for Larry. Please tell him he has an appointment with Pamela for 8:30 tonight. It would be good if he could get her to open up and let him in on her latest project. I'd tell him myself, but I think it will mean a lot more to him coming from her. Thank you. Bye!"

"They" can send each other cards and gifts for special occasions, too! Ordinary days become extraordinary when "Arnie" receives a love letter signed, "All my love, 'Shelley'"!

Just a recommendation: For obvious reasons, make sure you don't know anyone by these same names!

Who's the Boss?

One of your secrets as lovers is that you constantly consider each other's needs and try to anticipate each other's preferences. Typically, when you get stuck on a difference of opinion, you simply negotiate your way through to a mutually acceptable solution. Great! Keep up the good work.

Except...all that compromising and agreeability can sometimes get in the way of your powerful need to satisfy your lover's every desire. Could it be that she is holding back on something she would like to do with you sexually because she isn't sure whether or not you would enjoy it, too?

If you play "Who's the Boss?" every few weeks, it will help you to create the perfect environment for ferreting out one another's hidden needs and wishes. It will also give both of you "legal" permission to focus solely on your own needs for a day, without feeling that you are being selfish.

The weekend may be an ideal time to begin, since it takes 48 hours to play "Who's the Boss?" The rules are simple, but extremely effective:

1. Flip a coin to find out, "Who's the Boss?" on Day One.

2. The winner is required to set the first day's sexual agenda. Suppose your wife wins. That means she can do anything she desires to you, whenever she wishes, all day long. She can also ask you to do anything for her that strikes her fancy.

3. There is only one stipulation: It cannot be something that either of you has ever done with each other before!

4. Since your wife won the coin toss, you must cooperate fully and enthusiastically with every one of her instructions. Your wholehearted eagerness to please her will

communicate this message to your wife loudly and clearly:
"Darling, nothing is more exciting to me than exciting you!"

5. On Day Two, your roles reverse. All of the same rules apply. Your wife must now do whatever pleases you!

When your two days are up and the game is over, you will both have a deeper insight into the one-of-a-kind mate God gave you.

You will also return to your normal, "balanced" relationship with a curious peace, as though you have each struck a very deep chord within the other.

And that's what "games" are really for.

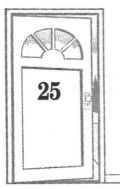

"Ten Magic Words" That Can Revolutionize Your Sex Life!

25

In the first Secret, we promised that we would show you how to bring up a sexual problem during your weekly one-hour appointment with each other (Doorway 18: "Is This the Time to Address Our Sexual Problems?").

We wanted to save this example until you had a chance to absorb the principles found in both Secrets. Now it is time to combine the two and to give you a glimpse into the power of that "synergistic effect" we described in our Introduction.

If your husband has been paying scant attention to your breasts in his lovemaking, you have a choice about how you can broach the subject. Of course the thing that is really bothering you is your fear that he no longer finds your breasts desirable. Certainly you can address that fear when you bring it up, but if you do it is going to come across as a complaint. As you learned in the first Secret, that approach seldom works.

You can say, "You never touch my breasts anymore. You used to caress them and kiss them until they were sore, but now you act as though they're not even there! Have they lost their shape? Are they not big enough for you now? Do I need to buy a bust exerciser, or what?"

That is, in fact, how some women would handle it. The fear of no longer being pretty enough to attract their husbands is pretty high on their list. They would allow their insecurity to dictate their approach.

But before you do the same, think it through. What would be the likely response from your husband? Thankfully, because he is your lover, you won't have to hear, "Well, Babe, let's face it. You ain't no spring chicken anymore. Know what I mean?"

Just the reverse will take place. As soon as your lover hears your fear, he will immediately shower you with reassurances. "Oh, Sweetheart! I love your breasts! They're precious to me. And they're beautiful—they really are! I'm sorry I haven't been paying attention to them. I had no idea! Well, you know, we've been rushed and everything lately, and I just haven't taken the time like I should. But don't worry, Darling, if you want sore breasts, from now on, you've got them!"

And you will. The very next time he makes love, you'll have to endure a mammary mauling that will make them ache for a week. But ask yourself this question: Is that really what you're after?

Not at all. You don't want to be pitied. You want his mind on making love, not on a gallant attempt to soothe your insecurity. You never did like having bruised breasts, and you still don't. What meant so much to you back then was that he was enamored with them.

But will his renewed attention tell you that now? Because of the way you brought it up, no it won't. The entire time he is handling your breasts, he will be thinking, "My poor baby. She's so worried that I don't like her breasts anymore. I hope this helps."

Well, phooey on that.

But it gets worse. Because at the same time you're thinking, "He's not doing this because he really wants to, is he? Of course he's not! He's doing it to make me feel better. But I don't. I feel worse!"

And you will. For how long? Oh, for ten or twenty years, maybe longer. Isn't that sad? For the rest of your lovemaking life, when your husband begins to touch your breasts you may have to put up with this nagging little voice way in the back of your mind, "Does he really want to do this— or is he just trying to spare my feelings?" The complaint approach backfires almost every time.

But the "backfire" is much worse when it comes to your sexuality. As lovers, you are triply sensitive there. Your love life is simply too important to handle with anything but the utmost tenderness, respect, and care. Never, never, never criticize your mate's performance in bed! And as you have just seen, it can be doubly lethal when you couple your complaint with fear.

Let me give you ten magic words. When you want something more or something different from your mate sexually, these loaded words create the perfect atmosphere for a favorable response. Here they are:

*Do you know what I would love
to try sometime?*

They sound simple, don't they? And they are. But with lovers, their effect is almost magical. When you say them with a sparkle in your eye, they accomplish two things. First, they create an atmosphere of expectancy, of excitement. They immediately get your spouse's attention and make his heart beat a little faster. When you ask him, "Do you know what I would love to try sometime?" it puts him on the edge of his seat and makes him want to answer with mounting excitement, "What? What? Hurry up and tell me!"

But secondly, and perhaps even more importantly, those ten magic words force you to present what you want positively, rather than negatively. They help you to rephrase your request in terms of your need or desire, rather than your complaint. You have called your mate to share an adventure!

Let's try it on your "breast request." When it's your turn during the hour, say to your husband, eyes dancing, "Let's talk lovemaking. Do you know what I would love to try sometime?" (And he's already going, "What? What?")

"I'd love for you to see how hot you could get me, just by making love to my breasts. Use your hands, your fingers, your lips, your teeth, your tongue—not roughly, but not too gently, either. As skilled a lover as you are, if you took your time and pulled out all the stops, I'll bet you could make me go absolutely wild!

"Unless, of course, you'd rather not have a wild woman in bed with you. I hear it puts quite a bit of strain on a man's heart! But Darling, there's no hurry. Whatever you do, don't try this until you think you can handle what may happen!

"Oh. And one other thing. When you decide to make love to me like that, don't call them "breasts." Call them—well, call them whatever you like. Maybe you can come up with a word that will be especially exciting for both of us."

Then sit back, smile at him sweetly, and when he can't talk for a moment because of the lump in his throat, you can say to him innocently, "Why, Sweetheart, what's wrong? 'Cat' got your tongue? I'm all through sharing my desire, Baby. Now it's your turn to share a need. Got a 'need' you want to share? Hmmmm?"

Now, that's the way to bring up a sexual problem! When you reword it as a desire, you are much more likely to enjoy the result. And in the future, your husband won't be paying attention to your breasts out of pity, either!

Just one word of caution: You might want to save your sexual requests for the end of the hour. Otherwise "something" may come up to interrupt your discussion and you may never get to the rest of the needs on your list!

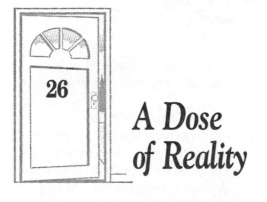

A Dose of Reality

One week before we mailed the manuscript of this book to our publisher, it was Judy's turn to lead the small-group women's Bible study she attends on Friday mornings. During their discussion, several of her friends expressed frustration at their inability to live up to the high standards portrayed by some Christian authors. Even worse, when they followed to the letter the advice written in some marriage manuals, they were acutely disappointed when their husbands did not respond in the way the authors predicted they would!

Judy's response was that some books can be very misleading. Sometimes, she pointed out, authors portray an exalted or impractical lifestyle that neither they nor any of their readers can hope to attain this side of heaven.

"What a disservice to their readers!" they all agreed. If a book paints an unrealistic picture of the day-to-day battle that is the Christian life, it can do more harm than good. Men and women will read this pie-in-the-sky fluff that the author invented out of whole cloth and feel defeated because they fall so far short of the apparent ideal.

And that was when one of the women asked only half-jokingly, "Is that the kind of book you and Steve are writing?"

The answer is "No." This book is not a crock. Judy and I are realists. We have personally experienced the oneness of body, mind, and spirit that we describe. We know what it is to be so close to the Lord and each other that we communicate almost intuitively. And yes, we are still groping for words to convey the inexpressible ecstasy God has allowed us to experience in earth-shattering, pane-rattling, no-limits lovemaking.

But that is not the whole story. The truth is, we hit more singles than we do home runs. And the absolutely gritty truth is that we have lost count of the number of times we have struck out.

Take for instance what happens every time I write a book on marriage. Satan becomes so furious at the good the book is going to accomplish that he launches an all-out attack on our marital relationship. At times during the writing, things get so bad between us that we find ourselves shaking our heads and asking each other if it is really worth it.

This happened during the writing of my book, *Tough Talk to a Stubborn Spouse*. Since its publication, millions have heard me share its principles on national talk shows such as "The Oprah Winfrey Show," "The Sally Jessy Raphael Show," and "The 700 Club." Hardly a week goes by that we don't hear about some marriage somewhere in the nation that was strengthened or saved through that book's influence. But during the time period when I was arising almost every morning at 3:59 to write it, there were times when, from the standpoint of our frayed emotions, Judy probably felt as though she thoroughly understood why some wives walk out on their husbands!

Having been through that once, we loaded up on lots of prayer and good intentions when we launched *For Lovers Only*. Well, it's a good thing we did. Because if we hadn't, I don't know what would have happened to Judith and Stephen Schwambach. So let me just give you a glimpse into what *did* happen!

A month after I began work on the book, the hard drive on my computer failed for the first and only time in five years. Although I constantly backed up all my work within the hard disk, I had neglected to make a totally separate copy. I was afraid I had lost everything.

"Not to worry!" said the computer repairman. "We can probably save all or at least most of what was on your disk."

And they did. They were able to save every single one of the hundreds of outdated, useless files and memos that I had stored on my hard disk and never got around to erasing. The only thing, in fact, that they were unable to save was my book. They lost it. Not some of it—all of it. After one month's work, I had not a single word to show for all my effort.

I spent two days in shock, walking about bumping into walls and mumbling to myself, "It's all gone. All of my book. It's all gone, that's all. It's just all gone." The good news is, that was when Judy offered to help me write the book. The bad news is, her offer made Satan twice as mad, which made him fight us twice as hard.

One of the ways she paid for her loving offer was that her seven-year off-and-on battle with panic attacks suddenly kicked into high gear. That meant a new barrage of tests, visits to several doctors, and a change of medication. As only panic attack sufferers can fully appreciate, it is somewhat difficult to concentrate on a book when your brain chemistry keeps screaming at you that you are about to die from a massive heart attack!

Next, our two youngest children, still at home, chose this delicate time of our lives to launch a three-month investigation into the joys of extreme hyperactivity.

Meanwhile, at the church I pastor, we were up to our ears in an aggressive fall campaign to expand our thrust as a caring community church. To top it off, my counseling load doubled and the phone rang at all hours of the day and night, as people who had read my first book reached out to me for help.

With the deadline looming ever nearer, there was nothing to do but take the writing time out of our sleep—and, quite stupidly, we would both now confess, out of our time with each other. As a result, we grew distant. There were times when, compared to our normal schedule, we felt like we hardly saw each other.

Four years ago, we had decided to extensively remodel our house. Many months ago, we selected an excellent Christian contractor and asked to be put on his schedule. Now please understand us. We were genuinely delighted when he had completed his promised projects for others and it finally became our turn. It's just that "our turn" came six weeks before our book was due! All day long, for five, sometimes six days a week, we have lived in a small corner of our house in the midst of falling plaster, dust everywhere, and the sounds of bumping, clanging, and incessant hammering in our ears. Half of our belongings are in boxes or stacked in odd places, which means that it takes us about a week to find something when we need it.

One day when my five-year-old Rebekah had about all of it she could stand, she asked me with genuine sincerity, "Daddy, why did you let those men chop down our house?"

At about the same time, one of our neighbors sent me a registered letter threatening to turn us in to the health department because of a leak in our septic system. But that was probably just a coincidence. Today—six weeks and many telephone calls and letters later—our septic system continues to leak, the odor is atrocious, and still we have not been able to hook up to the city sewer system! We're sure that's just a coincidence, too.

The last 11 days have been real precious. It all started on a Tuesday night when Abraham, our youngest, vomited in the van on the way home from an evening at Grandma's. Not to be outdone, Rebekah elected to empty the contents of her stomach during the night. One-by-one, we began falling like flies, until six out of the seven of us were lying around, moaning and groaning. If you count sore throats and stopped-up noses, all seven of us bit the dust. Did I mention the diarrhea, too? Oh, yes. We certainly wouldn't want to miss out on that, would we? We didn't.

No, this wasn't the 24-hour flu. It wasn't that 72-hour bug, either. At this moment we're at 254 hours and still going strong! Is this everything we have been through while writing this book? No, these are just the things we have not yet been able to repress.

Let me ask you a question: With the kids sleeping on the floor in our bedroom for the last six weeks, with our time alone together as a couple almost nonexistent, with our stress level near an all-time high, and with the encouraging sights, sounds, and fragrances of the intestinal flu our constant companion for lo, these many days—how do you suppose our sex life has been?

I don't think we've gone this long between lovemaking sessions in nearly 23 years of marriage. And yet, when my alarm goes off while it is still dark outside, I haul my aching carcass out of bed, pick my way through an obstacle course of sleeping bodies sprawled on the floor every which way in the dark, and stumble into the kitchen, where I rub the sleep out of my eyes, fire up our little lap-top computer, and extoll the joys of scintillating married sex! Half the time during this incredible ordeal, I've felt like the world's biggest liar.

But I'm not, and neither is Judy. We've been to the heights before and, by the grace of God, we'll be there again. Hopefully, by the time this book reaches your hands, we'll have taken a couple of exhilarating swings around Jupiter and Mars and be closer together as a couple than we've ever been. But right now, we make that confident prediction purely by faith.

On this particular Saturday, my family would rather be enjoying a relaxing van tour of the stunning fall foliage of southern Indiana. Instead, the kids are stuck in their half-remodeled home, while Mom and Dad furiously labor to finish their book on the joys of married life!

As you can see, Judy and I do not spend all of our time in outer space, exploring new worlds in our relationship. Sometimes we are stuck in mud two feet deep. This, dear reader, is also part of every lover's life in the real world.

As we finally bring this book to a close . . . Judy and I just wanted you to know.

Notes

Introduction
1. Philippians 3:12

Secret One

Doorway 3—Share Your Needs
1. Ephesians 4:29
2. Ephesians 4:2

Doorway 5—Don't Imply Blame
1. Ephesians 4:26

Doorway 9—Every Time a Problem Arises
1. Ephesians 4:26
2. Ephesians 4:27; Hebrews 12:15
3. Matthew 5:23,24

Doorway 13—You Do Not Need an Apology
1. Matthew 6:14,15
2. Luke 23:34
3. Luke 23:35-39

Doorway 26—Buy Some Time
1. Matthew 18:15-17
2. Colossians 3:5-10
3. Galatians 2:11-21
4. Ephesians 5:22-24; Colossians 3:18; 1 Peter 3:1-6
5. Matthew 23:2,3
6. Acts 5:27-29

Doorway 29—Lest You Misunderstand
1. Matthew 5:23,24

Doorway 30—This Isn't So Radical
1. Galatians 5:22-26
2. 1 Corinthians 13:4-8

Secret Two

Doorway 2—Please Read This First
1. Matthew 7:6
2. Acts 10:15

Doorway 3—How Far Can You Push It?
1. Matthew 25:21,23
2. Matthew 25:26
3. 1 Corinthians 9:8-10
4. Matthew 25:15

Doorway 4—But What Are the Rules?
1. Galatians 5:19-21; 1 Corinthians 6:12-20; Proverbs 5:1-14; 1 Thessalonians 4:3-5; Titus 3:3; Exodus 20:3; Ephesians 5:3,4; Deuteronomy 27:21; Romans 1:26,27; Matthew 5:28
2. Genesis 2:25

Doorway 5—What's Left? God's Very Best!
1. Proverbs 5:15-19
2. Song of Songs 1:2
3. Song of Songs 2:5
4. Song of Songs 2:16,17
5. Song of Songs 7:7-10

Doorway 7—God's Gift to His People
1. Galatians 5:1
2. John 10:10
3. Genesis 2:7
4. Genesis 2:24
5. James 1:16,17
6. Genesis 1:31
7. Psalm 8:3-6
8. Ephesians 5:28,29
9.. 1 Thessalonians 5:18
10. Romans 11:33-36
11. 1 Timothy 6:17
12. Mark 7:6-8
13. Galatians 5:24
14. Genesis 3:16
15. Psalm 20:4

Doorway 8—Why Did You Get Married, After All?
1. 1 Corinthians 7:1,2
2. 1 Corinthians 7:3,4
3. 1 Corinthians 7:5
4. Philippians 2:3,4
5. 1 Peter 3:1,7
6. 1 Corinthians 7:9
7. 1 Corinthians 7:12-20
8. 1 Corinthians 7:2

Doorway 13—Let Go of Others' Opinions
1. Genesis 2:24

Other Good
Harvest House Reading

TOUGH TALK TO A STUBBORN SPOUSE
by *Stephen Schwambach*

In the United States, someone gets divorced every 27 seconds. Nine times out of ten, only one of the partners wants a divorce, and it's the same one every time: the stubborn one. You may be that person. Perhaps you are the other spouse, or a child, or a relative or friend, but your heart is breaking because someone for whom you care deeply is headed straight for a divorce. What can you do?

Now you can give your loved one *Tough Talk to a Stubborn Spouse*. Author Stephen Schwambach pours 20 years of counseling and pastoring stubborn people into short, powerful chapters that will stimulate the thinking of husbands or wives. It could be the key that unlocks a desperate situation as Schwambach leads the reader through a last, hard look at their marriage.

QUIET TIMES FOR COUPLES
by *H. Norman Wright*

Noted counselor and author Norm Wright provides the help you need to nurture your oneness in Christ. In a few moments together each day you will discover a deeper, richer intimacy with each other and with God, sharing your fondest dreams and deepest thoughts—creating memories of quiet times togher.

GOOD MARRIAGES TAKE TIME
by *David and Carole Hocking*

Filled with teachings rooted in God's Word, this sensitive book offers help in four areas of married life: communication, sex, friends, and finances. Contains questions throughout the book for both husbands and wives to answer.

LIBERATED THROUGH SUBMISSION
by *P.B. Wilson*

As a strong woman married to a strong man, Bunny Wilson became angry and frustrated when she first heard that submission was the key to a fulfilled marriage. She chafed when she tried to understand Bible verses about it. Yet as she studied, she discovered there *was* more to submission than she realized. Submission was for everyone—every man, every woman, married or single.

In this provocative and surprising book, Bunny Wilson shares her clear and thoughtful understanding of a principal that could revolutionize the most important relationships in your life.

DATING YOUR MATE
by *Rick Bundschuh* and *Dave Gilbert*

If you've ever longed to return to those wonderful, fun-filled days of "courting," then *Dating Your Mate* is for you and your spouse. Chock-full of clever ideas that will put the romance, excitement, and spontaneity back in your life, *Dating Your Mate* is a practical guide to creative fun for marrieds and yet-to-be-marrieds. Delightfully illustrated by the authors.

ROMANTIC LOVERS
The Intimate Marriage
by *David and Carole Hocking*

Here is romantic love for married couples that exceeds our greatest dreams and expectations! Greater intimacy is possible as we follow God's beautiful picture of marriage as found in the Song of Solomon.